ISBN 978-0-267-67560-9
PIBN 10235242

This book is a reproduction of an important historical work. Forgotten Books uses
state-of-the-art technology to digitally reconstruct the work, preserving the original format
whilst repairing imperfections present in the aged copy. In rare cases, an imperfection in
the original, such as a blemish or missing page, may be replicated in our edition. We do,
however, repair the vast majority of imperfections successfully; any imperfections that
remain are intentionally left to preserve the state of such historical works.

KEPT IN

INDIA, EGYPT, AND SYRIA.

BY

THE VISCOUNTESS FALKLAND.

"And in his brain
———— ———— he hath strange places cramm'd
With observation, the which he vents
In mangled forms."—As You Like It.

IN TWO VOLUMES.

VOL. II.

Second Edition, Revised.

LONDON:
HURST AND BLACKETT, PUBLISHERS,
SUCCESSORS TO HENRY COLBURN,
13, GREAT MARLBOROUGH STREET.
1857.

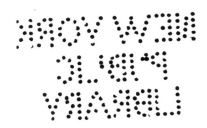

LONDON:
Printed by Schulze and Co., 13, Poland Street.

CONTENTS OF VOL. II.

CHAPTER V.

CHAPTER VI.

CHAPTER VII.

CHAPTER VIII.

CHAPTER IX.

CHAPTER X.

CHAPTER XI.

CHAPTER XII.

CHAPTER XIII.

CHOW-CHOW.

CHAPTER I.

THE WANDERING TRIBES OF THE DECCAN.

DURING the monsoon, and particularly near Gunes-kondy, we often see an encampment of wild-looking men, women, and still wilder, untameable, little children.

They are called Weyds, and are aboriginal, with a language distinct from all other Hindoo dialects. They carry about medicines for sale to the neighbouring villages. I have frequently met them on the plains, when they used to show me their medicines, principally powdered herbs—some in gourds, others in cocoa-nut shells.

VOL. II.   B

The little children are quite savage; necklaces of shells and beads are their principal covering. The scanty dress of the men is the colour of brick-dust, especially worn by those who worship Siva. In October and November they visit the hills to dig for medicinal roots, and collect the scales of the pangolin-manis—a scaly, lizard-shaped animal, about four feet long, very like a land-alligator.[1] These scales, as well as the medicines, are put into their wallets, and carried about the country for sale. Tigers' claws, also, when procurable, are esteemed a valuable addition to the stock of the wallet; a necklace of them round a child's neck is an in-fallible safeguard against the evil eye. Tigers' flesh is also a favourite specific, and large quantities of it are consumed in all diseases where medicine of a healing nature is required. It is also believed to pre-dispose to anger, and swallowed from a motive analogous to that of the running-footman, who ate hare to make him fleet. There is always sure to be, in some corner of the wallet, a small bottle or gourd full of tigers' fat—a sovereign

---

[1] The pangolin is an ant-eater, and digs for his food with huge claws, which give him a very formidable appearance, though he is perfectly harmless. He is covered all over wit a kind of armour, of triangular-shaped, horny scales, whic are said to be strong enough to turn a bullet.

remedy against all the infirmities of old age. The Weyds also carry quantities of jackal skins, which they sell to persons who believe them to be very efficacious in curing rheumatism.

The Weyds keep quite distinct from other classes in their marriages, which are performed by a gooroo—a lay priest of their tribe, who has often to be sent for from a great distance to perform the ceremony; after which the red powder, goolal, is profusely distributed, and a plentiful meal provided in which the chief article is frequently the flesh of jackals or foxes, for they are not nice in these matters.

There are several wandering tribes in the Deccan; but, next to the Weyds, the Bunjaras most attracted my notice. Passing an encampment of these people once, at the Mahabaleshwur Hills, I stopped to take a sketch of one of the women in her picturesque dress. The moment I began to draw, she fell into a fit of laughter, rolling herself in the dust, which did not improve her appearance; and whenever I endeavoured to take up the pencil again, she recommenced the laughing and rolling. I saw it was hopeless, so I went on my way, and no doubt she thought me as extraordinary as I did her.

The following details are taken from a

paper in the 'Bombay Literary Transactions,' en-
titled 'An Account of the Origin, History, and
Manners of the Race of Men, called Bunjaras,'
written by Captain Brigg :—

"It is generally known, that previous to the
Mahomedan invasion of the Deccan, in the fourteenth century, this part of India was divided into
five nations.

"Mountains, forests, and rivers without bridges,
separated these people, but still did not prevent
their mutual intercourse, and a constant traffic was
carried on between them ; thus, one tribe would
supply silks and cloth, which another purchased
with gold. Independently of trade in articles of
luxury, however, the nature of the country, of the
climate, and of the inhabitants of India, promotes
an intercourse essential to their very existence.

"The uncertainty of the periodical fall of rain is
frequently productive of famine ; and, in such a
case the only alternatives left for the people of one
part of the country, are either to emigrate to
another, or to have grain brought to them : the
latter, therefore, is naturally adopted, and has been
for ages carried on by the Bunjaras by means of
bullocks, which they are to be seen conductin
with their heavy burdens, either toiling up th

Ghauts, or leisurely traversing the plains from village to village.

"The leading bullock is generally a finer animal than his fellows, and is decorated with large tassels of red and black wool, and a bell; the monotonous jingle of which always announces the approach of a tribe of Bunjaras."

Bunjara is a compound Hindoo word, signifying 'burning the woods,' or 'living in the woods.' Captain Brigg thinks the latter, as 'bun,' or 'run,' means either a wood or waste.

When they halt they never put up in a village, but at some distance outside, and near water if possible. They pitch their camp of small tents, composed of a single web of cloth raised on a ridge by a cord supported between two short poles, and pegged down at the ends. The loads of the bullocks are piled in regular rows, and the bullocks driven out to graze; cooking, eating, and sleeping, occupy the afternoon, and towards evening the bullocks are brought in and piqueted in rows to strong pegs driven into the ground. Long before day-light the whole camp is astir. The tents are struck, the loads placed on the bullocks; the younger children set astride on the mother's hip, or tied in a cloth on her shoulder, and the whole 'Tanda,' as such an encampment is called, is in motion, and they travel on for ten or twenty miles, till the heat of the forenoon sun, or a suitable place for encamping, induces them to stop for the day.

Every ' Tanda' is under a ' naik,' or leader, who regulates its movements, and agrees with the merchants for the carriage of their goods. Their staple occupations are carrying grain, and cotton, down to the coast and bringing back salt, and bulky articles of foreign import. But, whatever goods may be entrusted to his care, it is said, that no Bunjara naik was ever known to betray his trust, or behave dishonestly with regard to the goods committed to his charge.

This people were divided into four classes, their manners, language and habits being quite distinct from the other tribes of the Deccan. They are certainly foreigners, and claim a Rajpoot descent, and it is probable they arrived with the Moguls when they invaded that country.

The costume of the women is peculiar—much more like what is seen in the sculptures of very old temples—than anything in the Hindoo habiliments of the present day. It is very picturesque. There is a boddice rather long in front, and a strong dark blue petticoat ; they wear many heavy massive rings of ivory round their arms and legs. The hair is knotted behind and tied with cowries, and red silk tassels, and sometimes gold or silver ornaments are suspended from the head. The men fasten their short trowsers round the waist with several gay coloured tassels. They are a remarkably finely made, handsome race, and there is frequently seen among them, what is rare in India, a brilliant high colour in the cheeks of the young people. The young women are often extremely handsome; but a life of exposure and severe toil soon makes them look coarse.

Their primitive, secluded, and independent mode of existence is very curious.

'In the rains' they are to be found among the deep grassy glens of Mysore, or Berar—in places where there are no inhabitants, and, consequently, no cultivation. In such situations they make themselves huts of boughs, or stretch out their small tents tightly, so that they may turn off the rain.

The cattle are let loose to graze, care being taken that two active young lads go with them, well-armed with a good serviceable spear, and accompanied, if possible, by a buffalo, for which this reason is assigned, that the buffalo will always run to the rescue of a man or beast, attacked by a tiger. This may seem incredible, but I knew of a case at the hills, when a herd of buffalos drove off a tiger who was about to seize one of the drove.

Two other well-attested cases have also been mentioned to me, in which the herdsman was attacked or threatened by a tiger, and rescued by his buffalos, which formed themselves into a compact body and charged the intruder.

The Bunjaras having disposed of their cattle by sending them out to graze, some busy themselves in weaving a strong cloth, which is used for grain bags, others seek the plant, *crotalaria juncea* (of which the cloth is made), which, when ripe by the end of the rains, is beaten out into fibre, to be worked up at leisure.

By the time the rains are over, the cattle are in a condition to receive their loads, and away they go towards the coast, taking with them some cows, as well as bullocks, and not unfrequently a stray pony or two, which gradually lose their proper horse pace, and assume the leisurely tread of the bullock. Till lately the cows were always exempt from carrying burdens, and old Bunjaras account for the decay of their trade and the supercession of the pack-bullock, by carts, and other new-fangled contrivances, as a judgment on their race, for their covetousness in not respecting the sacred character of the cow, and in using her as a common beast of burden.

High up in Nimar, between the rivers Nerbudda and Taptee, are some of the extensive wastes where the Bunjaras dwell, and where other people are afraid to make permanent abode, by reason of the malaria. That, however, does not affect the Bunjaras much, as they move off before the bad season in November and December.

They have one remarkable custom, that of keeping a *bard*, who recites the doings of their forefathers, and, at their great festivals, sings and plays on the guitar. This is one of their Rajpoot characteristics.

They keep large numbers of very handsome but fierce dogs, looking like rough, shaggy greyhounds, and can scarcely be prevailed upon to part with them. These dogs are used both to protect their property and for hunting, of which they are very fond ; men, women, and children all joining in the chase.

Among other wild-looking wandering people, were some who seemed to live for nothing but to go head over heels. Among them were often young women, generally with very beautiful figures, who were accompanied by men playing a small drum.

The women often run for some distance by the carriages of Europeans, every now and then performing 'soubresauts;' and overtaking the carriage again, they would re-commence these ungraceful gambols till they were quite breathless.

These people are, I believe, called 'Kolhatees.' Then, there are others, who go about with baskets of snakes. Among them is the cobra; this the men, when they see an European walking or driving, instantly take out of the basket, and throw into the middle of the road. Then, out of another basket jumps a *mun-goose*,[1] which seizes the snake, and a fearful battle follows; the snake bites the mun-goose, and the latter attacks the snake. The mun-goose squeals, and one thinks it is in the last agony; not at all; it gets away, runs off, and, as the owner asserts, seeks an herb, which entirely cures the wound it has received; though sceptical people declare that the fangs of the snakes which are trained for these exhibitions are always extracted beforehand. The mun-goose is a pretty little animal; it is kept as a pet, and as a protection against snakes, on which, in a wild state, it habitually makes war. These snake-

---

[1] An ichneuman, very like an ash-coloured ferret.

wallahs run also by the side of carriages, holding up a snake's head, and calling out for 'pice.' [1] Men, leading bears, are often seen attended by a goat and a monkey or two. In stations where European officers or any government officials are to be found, they usually content themselves with making the unhappy bear dance and perform antics; but I have heard of their using the bear, in remote villages, to terrify the peasants, and extort money, by making it stand sentry at the door of a house till the inmates complied with the owner's demand, and induced him to move on. A degree of tyranny nearly equal to that exercised by the owners of barrel-organs in our own country.

It would be an endless task to enumerate all the half-wild and vagabond tribes, which lead a kind of gipsey life, in the plains of the Deccan, where there is never any heavy rain to force them to seek better shelter than is afforded by the rude tents or mat-huts in which they live. I am sorry to say most of them have but an indifferent reputation for honesty, and so formidable were the depredations of some classes, that the same department which had been organized under Colonel Sleeman to suppress

[1] A small coin.

Thuggee, was employed when Thugs [1] became scarce, to trace out the system of gang-robbery, by which many of these tribes subsisted; and the officers have been as successful against the robbers as they were against the murderers. One of the officers drew up a list of the wandering and other predatory tribes, in the habit of infesting the districts of the Bombay Presidency, with their occupation both ostensible and real. [2] It was printed by government as an official paper.

He enumerates no less then seventy-one such distinct tribes, and I am assured that he has by no means exhausted the catalogue.

These tribes neither intermarry nor interfere with each other's peculiar pursuit, which is too often some form of robbery; some rob only by night,

---

[1] I once saw at the hills several Thug "approvers" who had been pardoned, and were employed by the Government as agents in the suppression of Thuggee. I heard one of these men own to having committed one hundred murders. He was anxious to exhibit before me his mode of casting the noose. This I declined witnessing, remembering a story I had heard of a gentleman at Bombay having allowed himself to be made a *sham* victim; but unfortunately the Thug pulled the handkerchief rather too tightly, and the poor gentleman half suffocated called out in agony to be released from his peculiar and painful position.

[2] Vide paper by Captain Harvey, in the Police selections from the records of government, Bombay, 1853.

others invariably by day; some commit burglaries, others only petty thefts; one tribe confines itself to picking pockets, another to some peculiar form of swindling. Thus a tribe is mentioned as distinguished by all the women being thieves, who rob in regular gangs, under their female leaders, while the men are ostensibly basket-makers, and are left at home to perform the household duties of cooking and tending the children. The real jugglers known as Yergolhs or Golhurs are said not to be professional thieves, but go about exhibiting tricks, many of which would attract attention, by their cleverness, even in a London theatre. A very common one, is to plant the stone of a mango tree in a pot which is covered up, and when uncovered is found to contain a small mango tree with fruit on it. A boy is tied up in a net, thrust into a basket and covered over with a blanket, when the blanket is removed the boy is gone, and answers when called from a neighbouring field or from a tree. This of course is done by ventriloquism. It is not only that some of the tricks are very good, but the whole apparatus is so very simple. There is no stage, no carefully managed artificial light. The juggler attracts attention by a few taps on a small drum, or a note or two on a rude pipe; a person goes out to see what is the matter, and returns with the request that the juggler may be allowed to show off a few tricks for the amusement of the people of the house, and if leave be granted, the artist sets down his bags and baskets containing all his ' stage properties,' and after a few preliminary tumbles or tricks with cups and balls, proceeds to show off his feats of legerdemain on the gravel-walk in front of the verandah.

I will conclude this chapter with an account of the Bohras and Khojas, although they are not wandering wild tribes. The word 'Bohra' means 'merchant.' All real Bohras are Mussulmans; they are often pedlers; therefore, pedlers are popularly known as Bohras, just as old-clothes men are set down as Jews: but the name properly belongs to a peculiar sect of Mahomedans, looked on by others as heretics. Many Banians of the Jain sect follow the same calling as the regular Bohras, but they have no right to the name. These pedlers have shops in the bazaars, but almost every day you see them coming slowly up to the European bungalows, followed by men, often by women, carrying large baskets and boxes, in which are a variety of goods. They generally go to a back-door, as they are very much protected by ayahs and ladies'-maids, who look forward to the Bohras' visit with as much satisfaction as the gentleman of the house does the contrary. The maid is sure to tell her mistress she wants something, and that something, whether a yard of tape, or ten of broad-cloth, is sure to be at the bottom of the last box; so the lady and her maid have the satisfaction of seeing the contents of five or six boxes. In them is everything, from a Delhi shawl embroidered in gold, to a piece of Welsh flannel, but not all indis-criminately packed up together.

There is, however, one basket called '*chow-chow*,' which literally means a mixture—in fact, 'hodge-podge' or "odds and ends"—and in it is contained a mass of mingled objects, good, bad, and indifferent, something like the subjects of this book, the two latter probably predominating.

"Lady Sahib want fine cheese? here 'Uncle Tom's Cabin,' (which the Bohrah had just purchased at a sale). I got good pickle. There box of French gloves. Take soap, Lady Sahib?" Then he tempts the lady's maid with a gay ribbon, and by degrees, the contents of the chow-chow basket are displayed. Side by side stand a bottle of anchovy sauce, and one of tincture of rhubarb. There lies a Wiltshire cheese, surrounded by Goa lace, English tapes, and French ribbons. There are bottles of ink, blacking and hair-dye in the neighbourhood of fringes, pins and needles. There are gum and gauzes lower down; tooth brushes; flannel jackets and cigars; deeper and deeper are found more treasures, till at last the contents of the basket are exhausted; and after the Bohra has shown his numerous goods, all ends in half-a-yard of ribbon being bought for Madame Sahib's cap!

The goods are then replaced, all is packed up, the boxes put on the men and women's heads again, and they all move off patiently, and without grumbling; and what is still more extraordinary, leave the mistress and lady's maid quite exempt from any qualms of conscience, at having given the poor people so much trouble.

It is very difficult to learn anything certain about the history of the Bohras, or their doctrines, partly because they are peculiarly reserved, and averse to tell strangers about themselves, but more from their general ignorance of all matters unconnected with trade.

A Bohrah, with any pretension to learning, is not to be met with; and their priests, or Moollahs, are as ignorant as the laity.

They are most commonly met with in Western

India, near the coast from Cutch to Goa; scattered colonies are found in most large towns on the coast of Arabia and Persia. About Broach, and the Gulf of Cambay, they hold land, and are as thrifty and industrious in cultivating it, as their commercial brethren are in trading.

Their head-quarters are at Booranpoor, on the Tapty, near Asseerghur and Surat, where their head Moollah lives. Their doctrines are but little known, but they are generally regarded by the more orthodox sect, as partaking of the Ismalite heresies; and like the Kojas, believe their Aga to hold the keys of heaven, so that no Bohra can enter paradise without a certificate or passport from him. This passport is given literally, and in a tangible sheet of paper, specifying the heavenly inheritance reserved for the deceased. A large sum of money is paid to the Moollah for this paper, which is buried with the corpse, and is believed by the lower orders, at all events, to be necessary to save the deceased from a kind of purgatory.

There are different opinions as to the country from whence they originally came. It has been asserted that, from their features, genius, and manners, they are of Jewish origin. There are others who believe they came originally from

Turkish Arabia, or Syria, driven out by persecution for their heretical opinions.

About twenty years ago, a great fire broke out in Surat, and it is affirmed that whole families of women and children perished in the flames, rather than save their lives by exposing themselves in the public streets. This gives some idea of the more than Oriental seclusion in which they live.

When the Bohras pray, they wear an appropriate dress, which is daily washed.

The Kojas are a kindred tribe of Mahomedan heretics. They do not usually, like the Bohras, travel about as pedlers, but in Bombay, and other seaport towns of Western India, and in Cutch, they have a great share in the local trade ; and in Scinde, where they are very numerous, I am told they cultivate land, and are distinguished for their enterprise and industry. They are said to be converted Hindoos, and their religion (of which very little is known), to be a strange mixture of Mahomedanism, and mysticism, partly of Hindoo origin, partly derived from Syrian sources. But their chief peculiarity is their devotion to their 'Aga,' or lord, who is the spiritual head of all the Mahomedan sects, which are tainted with the 'Ismalite' heresy. He is the lineal descendant of the chief, who, as sheikh of the tribe of Hassassins, gave a new name to the crime of secret murder, and who, because most Sheikhs were old men, became so fatally well known among the Crusaders, as ' the old man of the mountain.'

The present Aga is connected, by marriage, with the Royal Family of Persia, and some years ago aspiring to the throne, was defeated, and fled to Candahar, where he and his " free lances" took service under General Nott. He came to Scinde with General England, and served under Sir Charles Napier at the conquest of that province, from whence he meditated another attempt on the Persian throne ; but this time little followed beyond diplomatic notes between our government and that of Persia, which led to the Aga being told that if he wished for an asylum in our territory, he must not levy war against our neighbours. Since then he has lived principally at Bombay, drawing a large revenue from his rich disciples in those parts, who pay him an obedience almost as absolute as that shown to his ancestors in the times of the Crusaders ; though it is now shown by paying heavy tithes on all the earnings of an industrious people, instead of by assassinating any one who may be obnoxious to the Aga or his tribe.

CHAPTER II.

ONE year, being on our way to Daporie, from the Hills, at the commencement of the monsoon, we visited Sattara. I had long wished to see the capi- tal of Sivajee, the great founder of the Mahratta empire, where he and his descendants lived at first, as the real rulers of the Mahrattas, and afterwards as nominal sovereigns, while the real power was usurped by their Peishwa, or Prime Minister.

Our visit took place during the interregnum between the death of the Rajah, and the decision of the Home Government on the subject of the adoption.

During this interval of suspense, the eldest of the Rajah's three widows was regarded as head of the Royal house, and did the honours of the Court to visitors.

As we began our journey in palanquins down the Ghaut, we were overtaken by a violent thunder-storm. The bearers, happily, could not be wet through, having but little covering.

We quitted the palanquins below the Ghaut, and got into carriages. The roads—never good—were unusually bad. Once the wheels stuck fast in the mud and sand, out of which the carriage was dragged by dint of whipping the poor horses most unmercifully, and the loud shouting of the coach-man urging the animals on.

Presently, one of our party rode by, calling out that he and his horse had been rolling in the mud; and, from their appearance, this could not be doubted. We went on far from prosperously, doing but eighteen miles in four hours.

When it became finer, towards the evening, F— rode on to Sattara. I arrived late. It was dark; but, whenever it lightened, I could see crowds of natives in white; then, between the salutes, I heard the tinkling bells of many elephants. I knew now the governor had arrived; and, under agreeable

auspices, as he had brought the monsoon with him
—for the native seers of Sattara disliking the an-
nexation of their country to the British territories
—had prophesied that, in consequence of (what
they thought) so great an injustice having been
committed before high Heaven, the usual rains
would not fall this year, and that a famine would
ensue.

Mr. Frere, now commissioner in Scinde, was
at that time commissioner at Sattara. We remained a few days on a visit at his house, and I
always look back to the time passed in his and
Mrs. Frere's society with real pleasure.

The situation of the town of Sattara is beautiful,
in one of those magnificent Deccan plains nearly
surrounded by mountains; and·above the town is
the fort, standing on a hill some hundred feet in
height. It was built by Sivajee, and in it is still
shown the palace in which his descendants were
for so many years imprisoned by their nominal
ministers, the Brahmin Peishwas.

The fort contained no less than sixteen temples,
of which four were dedicated to different forms of
Siva, or Mahadeo, the tutelary god of the Mahratta race; and five to various shapes of the dread
goddess Bowanee, the patroness of Sivajee and his

families. Two of these temples were especially dedicated to her, who is, as I have already remarked,
the goddess of small-pox and cholera.

Most of the garrison establishments of the hill-
forts are hereditary. I have a list of the hereditary office-bearers of Sattara fort as they stood at
the time we were there; all of them asserted that
their office had been originally conferred on their
ancestors by Sivajee. The garrison muster-roll
may have some interest, as illustrating the military
arrangements of bygone days. It comprised the
families of a washerman, a tailor, a potter, a smith,
a carpenter, a sword cutler, an astrologer, a pen-
man, a Mahomedan moolla or priest, a goldsmith,
and a gardener! All of these had small patches
of land assigned to them for their subsistence.
Near the fort in which they all lived, seventeen
families of Mhars had not only land, but six shil-
lings a month each in cash—a rare privilege in the
garrison; and they had also a priest of their own,
with a separate stipend: so had thirty families of
hereditary Mahratta sepoys, and two ensign-
bearers, who, with the Mhars, formed the fighting
portion of the garrison.

It is a tradition current in the hill-forts in the
Deccan, and so universally so that it can hardly

be destitute of some foundation in fact, that human sacrifices were always a part of the ceremony of laying the foundations of a hill-fort. There can be no doubt that such sacrifices were a part of the religion of the aboriginal inhabitants of the Deccan, and numerous traces may yet be found of the prevalence of such bloody rites.

At Sattara, the tradition runs that the son and daughter of the head Mahr[1] of the district were buried alive under the towers which flank the principal entrance to the fort, and similar tales are told of the other towers.

It is not, then, to be wondered at, that the Deccan forts are supposed to be peopled with ghosts. The chief object of the rites practised by the Mahrs, at the dussera, is to appease these spirits.

[1] The Mahrs and Mangs are 'outcast,' and live apart, generally outside the fort or village walls. They are supposed to be remnants of a conquered race, reduced to the condition of helots by the conquering Hindoos. Among themselves (as I have said in my account of the palanquin-bearers, who are of the Mahr caste) they always assume the title of aborigines. Large numbers of them were always attached to each of the hill-forts, and a cluster of their huts will generally be found in some sheltered spot at the foot of the hills within gun-shot of the fort walls. They not only did most of the service of the garrison in cutting and carrying grass, fire-wood, and other burdens, but took a prominent part in the defence of the stronghold whenever occasion required.

A gentleman of my acquaintance was present on the night of this great festival, and gave me the following details of what took place: "A young bull-buffalo was brought up to the temple of Bowanee, the tutelary goddess of the, fort, the patroness of Sivajee its founder, and the female incarnation of evil and all that is cruel and sanguinary. The temple stands near the angle at which tradition says several thousand of the besieging troops of Aurungzebe, the Emperor of Delhi, were destroyed by one of their own mines, 'through the special interposition of the goddess.' It is a small stone temple, of the ordinary form. Inside, when we reached it, were several Mahr priests engaged in ceremonies of which we could see but little by. the light of a single lamp. Outside were crowds of Mahrs—some holding the buffalo by ropes tied to the horns, others armed with old swords and spears. 'It is but a calf,' said an old man near me; 'there is nothing done now as in the old time, when we used to have the largest and finest bull-buffalo in the whole country to sacrifice.

"Presently, one of the priests from within the temple came out, and the chief Mahr present stepped forward and struck the animal a slight blow on the neck, with a sword. There is always some dispute between the heads of rival houses for the honour of striking the first blow; but, when once struck, every one present rushed at the poor beast, which was allowed, by those who held the ropes, to run to the narrow path, which follows the course of the ramparts round the crest of the precipitous hill. The whole crowd followed, yelling and striking the victim with their weapons, if they had any, or, if unarmed, with their hands. From what I heard, they seemed to have some notion like that attached to the scapegoat; the striking the animal transferred to it, not their sins, but their *ill-luck*, as they called it. Terrified by the noise and blows, the poor creature was not long in running the circuit of the ramparts; and, when it returned to the temple, it was dragged, bleeding and exhausted, to the temple-door, where its head was struck off by a blow from the sword of one of the principal Mahrs, and the whole crowd set to work to cut up the carcase.

"I had not expected anything so savage as the whole scene; and went to bed to dream of these cruel rites in the old palace fort. When about midnight, I was aroused by a sort of dirge, in which one voice chaunted a sentence, after which a chorus replied, and so on, in alternate verses. It was the whole body of the Mahrs going round the fort in solemn procession, and chanting an invocation to the ghosts and demons to come and accept the offerings for them.

" These offerings consisted of pieces of the flesh of the victim—of the blood which had been caught in a dish, when the head was struck off—of bread—of intoxicating spirits—of every eatable in common use among the Mahrs—salt—sugar—spices—ghee —opium—and tobacco—all were borne on brass or copper dishes, and surrounded by men carrying naked swords.

" The entrails of the victim were wound round the necks of the elders of the tribe who led the way.

" It is impossible to give a perfect impression of the wild and unearthly effect of the chant, as the procession passed slowly round the ramparts.

" The following translation of some of the sentences I heard, may give some idea of its character. It began with a sort of dialogue :—

> Solo.—' Beat, lads, beat !
> Chor.—Strike, lads, strike !
> Solo.—Strike with a club !
> Chor.—What shall we strike !
> Solo.—Strike the foeman !'

(Then, after repeating several sentences of the same kind, the invocation of demons began).

  Solo.—‘ Drop by drop,
    Drink blood !

  Chor.—Drink blood !

  Solo. — Bit by bit,
    Eat flesh !

  Chor.—Eat flesh !’

 Each of the following sentences were repeated in chorus after the solo :

  Solo.—‘ Take some liver !
    Eat some bread !
    Taste the gore !’

 And so on, through the whole list of the barbarous feast; as each article was named, a morsel of it was taken from the dish on which it was carried, and thrown into the air, over the rampart, and was supposed to be taken by some of the crowd of spirits who were believed to hover round the assemblage. After every two or three sentences, the whole body joined in a shout of ‘ Be propitious !’

 “ An old man, next day, told me—‘ We throw the morsels to the spirits. In former days, they used to be very bold, and came to take them out of our hands; now they are become more shy, and we must throw the morsels over the ramparts ; but still, not a morsel falls to the ground, all are caught up in the air as they fall ; and if you now go round under the path we traversed last night, you will not find a single morsel, nor the vestige of one. The spirits are still very dangerous to the impious, or unwary; and woe to the man who, from indolence, or a desire to pry, remains behind his fellows. Unless we all keep close round the dishes on which the offerings are borne, and the swordsmen hedge us round about, evil is sure to befal us. The danger is greater to a stranger than to one of ourselves; the demons know all of us who belong to the fort, and are less apt to hurt us; but a man from another village must be very careful. It was only last year, a relation of my own came here, a village four miles off, to see me at the Dussera. He was incautious, and lagged behind the main band, what he saw we know not, but he never reached his home alive. He set out to return next morning, and was seized and died on the road. The effect of the offerings is to propitiate the Demons for the rest of the year. After a while they become hungry again, and, if not propitiated, would possess us and our cattle."

The rain was constant during our stay at Sattara. I was rarely able to go out; but, whenever there was a 'break,' I hurried forth, and went one evening to Sungum Maolee, where the rivers,

Yenna and Crishna join. On both sides of the streams are several temples; and on the bank of the river on the Sattara side, are magnificent banyan trees, where wild monkeys live in luxury, fed carefully by the villagers; these animals are of the large kind, with grey beards.

On a very high bank overlooking the river, are temples, and a broad flight of steps leading up to them from the water's edge. The temples are built of stone in the usual style, some erected by private individuals, and dedicated to their favourite deities. One being in honour of Pureshram. In the ' Pooran,' which contains the marvellous deeds of Crishna, it is related that Pureshram was for several days under a Wur tree (Ficus indica), in the village of Maolee, performing religious austerities; on which account, the place is said to be sacred to him, and one who paid him a peculiar worship, built the temple here, one hundred and seventy-five years ago. Then there is another dedicated to the river gods, by a devotee, who conceived that ' as the Crishna and Yenna rivers are essences of the deity,' an edifice ought to be raised in their honor. All the temples have some tale or legend attached to them—one more will suffice.

" The temple dedicated to Rameshur was built

about eight years ago, by a man named Pureshram, who had formerly been a mendicant in Sattara. One day, as he was performing his religious duties near his hut, he saw a hole in the earth, and discovered a large cavity filled with treasure. He covered up the hole, and afterwards built on the spot a small cottage. Having managed to get out the treasure, he began to carry on the business of a banker with the cities around Sattara. The Rajah of Sattara, having at length heard of the above circumstance, sent for him, and, having learned from Pureshram himself the particulars of what had occurred, said to him—'The treasure which God has given you is yours, and you may safely enjoy it.' From that day Pureshram began to transact his business openly in Sattara itself."

This story is well known. Besides temples, Pureshram constructed dhurmsalas, wells, and other works, at an outlay of many lacs [1] of rupees.

There are several handsome tombs at Sungum Maolee, raised to the memory of widows who have performed suttee. Not far from these monuments is one to Shahoo Maharajah's black dog. The cause of its having been so highly honoured is this: "Shahoo Maharajah was very fond of hunting. He

---

[1] A lac is £10,000.

had a black greyhound named ' Kundia,' which one
day saved his life from a tiger, which was about
to spring upon him, and to which the dog, by
barking, drew his attention. The maharajah fired
at and killed the beast, and regarding the dog as
the preserver of his life, treated him ever after
with extreme kindness, taking him in his palanquin
whenever he went out. When the dog died, he
was buried at Maolee, and a monument was
erected on the spot.

One evening the Ranees of Sattara invited the
governor to a ' kutha ' (theatrical entertainment)
and ' natch.'

It was dark when we reached the palace; all
along the building were strings of lighted lamps.

On arriving, the youth adopted by the late
Rajah to succeed him on the musnid (throne), received Mrs. Frere and me at the great gate, and
we began a long walk through broad and narrow
passages, being preceded by men bearing torches;
then passing the large, dimly-lighted durbar-room,
mounted a very narrow dark staircase, and found
ourselves in a small apartment, where the ranees
met us, and after the customary salutations, we all
sat down on sofas. The governor and his suite had
not yet arrived; I had, therefore, a little time to

observe all around me. There were the three Ranees in beautiful sarees of rich, thick material, completely concealing them. Behind them stood several women, with chowries (largs fans made of peacocks' feathers, mounted in silver handles), and one held a silver box for the betle-nut, paun, and lime, which the Hindoos are constantly putting into their mouths. Native gentlemen, whose rank did not entitle them to sit on chairs, were either standing or sitting on the ground, numerous attendants being dispersed about.

The room was small. On each side were rows of wooden pillars, painted dingy red, and between them red silk curtains fastened up. There were openings into side apartments, before which hung red draperies. If there were windows in the room where we sat, they were closed. The heat was very great: the hanging lamps were numerous, and the wax candles in them were constantly going out.

When the Governor was announced, the Ranees met him at the door. The conversation was soon exhausted. Some of the family curiosities were brought. Among them Sivajee's sword, which he called 'Bhowanee,' after the goddess: it is now worshipped as a divinity, and has its own temple in the palace, with the usual allowance of well-paid Brahmins to perform the customary cere-monies of the shrine. It is curious that it is not an Oriental, but an Italian blade, of admirable tem-per and workmanship, with the word 'Genova,' and part of the maker's name still legible on it. The gentlemen of the party declared it was a very fine blade, of the kind sometimes shown in old Scotch collections as 'a real Andrea Ferrara.' With it is shown the sword of Afzool Khan, the unfortunate Beejapoore general, so treacherously murdered by Sivajee, which was taken from him by Sivajee at the time of the murder, and several varieties of 'wagnuks' (tigers' claws), and even the very one which Sivajee stuck into Afzool Khan's side. This I thought a very curious family treasure and relic; but I was told that Sivajee pretended, and his family affect to believe, that the murder was committed under the direct inspiration of his tutelary divinity, Bhowanee; and it was in truth a deed worthy of the sanguinary goddess, the guardian deity of Thugs, professed murderers.

We were shown some old pictures painted two hundred years ago by native artists: the subjects were different events in the life of Sumbajee, the son of Sivajee. The eldest Ranee displayed her girdle—a gold belt inlaid with precious stones, and one enormous emerald in the clasp. All the treasures ended with her highness's horoscope. It seemed to be an endless story—a long roll written in Sanscrit, and full of astrological figures; on the margin were illuminated patterns; at the commencement of the roll was a painting of Gunputty, the god of prosperity.

It was now time for the concert; the musicians sat on the ground. One had a large instrument shaped like a harp, but placed across his knees. It had a great number of strings. The sound was not unpleasant, and the performance was admirable. Another had a kind of violin, by no means agreeable to listen to. Then a third brought forth some very soft notes from a lyre, and a fourth played very expertly on a drum. The instrumental concert concluded, women came forward, sat down on the ground, and began singing. The prima donna's voice was very monotonous. She sang a solo, in Mahratta; other women joined in a chorus, the words of which, I was told, were, 'After twelve years send me back my love.'

I began to think this song would never end—so did the Ranee; she sent one of her attendants to desire the women not to be so slow, when the prima donna turned round to him, and said, "What do you know about music?" then went on with her singing till some 'natch' girls appeared.

I have described their manner of dancing already. They were beautifully dressed. The entertainment concluded with the Kuthas. The performer was a famous Hurdass Gossein, one of the most celebrated of his profession; while singing these kuthas, he struck together two large and very heavy pieces of bell-metal, which he held in one hand, somewhat in the manner of castanets. The sound is very agreeable, like the clear note of a bell. The subject of his first song was, Crishna going to battle and wanting water; he performed a miracle, and obtained some. The performance ended with a discourse on humility.

By this time it was getting late; the heat was almost intolerable. The candles were burning down fast; the mosquitos were devouring us; and it was time to retire, which we did, after expressing to the Ranees the gratification the evening's amusement had given us.

We then went through the same narrow passages again, the Governor holding Venkajee's hand, he taking one of mine, while my other hand was grasped by the youngest boy—so we all went along sideways (for the passages were too narrow to admit of four persons walking abreast), till we got to the carriages.

But there was still another festivity to take place the next day, for the Ranees had invited us to a cutcherry or durbar; and, on this occasion, their highnesses were to receive the Governor in state.

We went, in the first instance, to what is called the little palace, which is, in fact, a summer-house, situated in a garden; on entering which, we proceeded along a narrow, raised walk; on each side were ereca palms and cypresses, the light and graceful stem of the former contrasting with the dark foliage of the latter tree.

The little palace was nearly surrounded by a small tank, illuminated on all sides. The interior of the building was brilliantly lighted from top to bottom. One room was entirely encrusted with mirrors; even the ceiling; which had a curious effect, owing to the incessant multiplication of every light and object in the apartment. The ceiling of another chamber was painted vermilion, with a little gilding; the pillars being also of red. There were numerous examples of the Hindoo taste for decorating the walls of their dwellings with pictures and engravings, most frequently of the commonest sort, as they do not know the difference between a Claude and a one-shilling wood-cut. In one instance, the walls were covered with paintings, apparently copied from common English prints. They were on glass, and done in china, so crowded, that the frames touched each other; and were placed with little or no reference to the subject. Modern kings and heroes, ancient gods and goddesses of Greece or Rome, and Hindoo deities, all being mixed together.

I was much amused by observing the device employed to obtain space for one picture; there had evidently been no room for it in its proper position. The subject was a Venus lying down. The person who had arranged this curious gallery, would not leave the goddess out, and she was so placed, that she appeared standing on her head!

It was now time to go to the principal palace—where the Ranees expected the Governor. The building was surrounded by rows of lamps, and the street illuminations were managed in a very primitive manner—a number of small wicks were placed in little pans of oil, fixed on poles. There were crowds of natives, and several elephants were drawn up when we left the carriage. We were conducted into a large room, brilliantly lighted with coloured lamps. Here a supper was ready—half European—half Indian in the arrangements.

We were almost immediately told that the Ranees wished to receive the ladies. We had not far to go, for I heard the princesses were established in an inner apartment, with a bamboo screen suspended before the door. Behind this, the ladies and I therefore retired, and found ourselves in a dark room, when I was made conscious of the presence of the Ranees by one of them taking my hand and leading me to a sofa.

A few minutes only elapsed before a woman made her appearance, holding a common tin candlestick in which was a lamp. I could just perceive the eldest Ranee was unveiled. She seized my hand, and we began groping our way out of the room. The other Ranees and ladies followed—not a word was uttered. At first we traversed long dark passages, then hurried up and down steep, narrow staircases; when the way became too narrow, the Ranee and I were obliged to separate, and follow each other; when it became wider, she took my hand, and quickened her pace. On we went, the faint light of the attendant con-

stantly flickering before us, and we often lost sight
of her as she kept twisting and twirling among the
never-ending passages. At last we suddenly came
to the brink of a tank, surrounded by lights. Here
we halted. I began to think we were in an enchanted palace, and that the Ranee might disappear
on a broomstick. I had just time to breathe and
look at her: there she stood, at the edge of the
tank, looking rather more like a witch than a fairy.
I could see her neck was completely covered with
emeralds and pearls, her ancles with splendid ban-
gles, and her wrists and fingers glittered with bracelets and rings; while her highness's feet had not
been forgotten—for her toes were likewise adorned
with silver rings.

Again, quicker than ever, we seemed to fly
through more places of mystery, till we arrived,
unexpectedly, at the top of a staircase, where she
left me. I looked around, and, lo! she had
vanished! Below was a blaze of light, and the
voices of hundreds of human beings were distinctly
heard.

In a minute or two, her highness returned enveloped in a very ample and splendid saree, as were
also the two other widows. Again she took my
hand, and we went down the stairs, and entered

the durbar-room—the Ranee walking slowly, and in a dignified manner, through lines of courtiers and numerous attendants, ranged to receive her. The Governor and his suite were present.

The apartment was a fine one. The walls and pillars were covered with red silk and gold drapery, (Kincob) The chandeliers and lamps, which seemed countless, were of all kinds of coloured glass. On the floor were placed two very large silver candelabra. On one side of the room sat the European guests; on the other, the Hindoo court. The Ranees and the Governor occupied one end of the room, and close to the walls stood, or squatted down, crowds of natives.

Then followed the usual attempt at conversation, on the part of the Ranee; and the customary enquiries concerning our health, and whether our journey had been agreeable. Before we took leave we were shewn the private temple of the Ranees. The household gods were of gold, and surrounded by silver candlesticks.

Connected with this family temple, and the household gods, a story was told me which curiously illustrates the superstitions of even the upper classes of natives, and as it was related to the resident by the late Rajah's prime minister, and confidential friend, there can be no doubt of its truth. When the late Rajah felt his end approaching, as he had no children of his own ; he began to think seriously of adopting a successor. His own feelings were strongly in favour of adopting the little foundling-boy whom he had brought up as a kind of pet ; but to this step, considerations of family interest and policy were alike opposed, as the adoption of a child of low birth totally unconnected with his race, would greatly lessen the chance of the adoption being approved of by the government.

One day his prime minister, an old and faithful servant, happened to be *tête-à-tête* with his prince, and urged him so strongly on the point, that the Rajah said he would refer the matter for the decision of Bhowanee, hereditary tutelary deity of his house. So they went into the family temple, and the Rajah, taking some grains of boiled rice from the dish set before the idol, stuck one on each side of the image, saying, if the grain on one side stuck longest, he would consider it as approving his wish to adopt the foundling ; but if the grain on the other side adhered, he would be convinced his wish was disapproved of. The result was unfavourable to his pet, and the Rajah found out some reason for not thinking the test conclusive, and

evaded any final decision on the point. As, however, he daily got worse, and the people around
him pressed him to adopt some one, he again sent
for the prime minister, and, when they were alone,
made him write on two slips of paper the name of
his pet, and that of a distant blood relation of his
highness' own. These papers were folded, thrown
down on the floor before the idol, and a young
child, who was playing in the street, was called
in and told to go into the temple, pick up one
piece of paper and bring it to the Rajah. This was
done, and the paper bore the name of the blood
relation. The Rajah then bowed to fate and
Bhowanee, and adopted his relative; and, though
the issue of the matter was not such as he hoped
for, he consoled himself by thinking that it was,
at all events, the will of Bhowanee and a decree
of inexorable fate.

The following day we left Sattara in a storm,
and passed the next twenty-four hours in our carriages. Our journey was retarded by the overflowing of the rivers, the rain having fallen inces-
santly for several days.

We found, during our journey, only one bridge
over the Crishna. When we reached the sacred
stream at other places, we had to ford it. At one

spot the water was so high that it entered the carriage; and when we reached the other side, the water had to be baled out. I thought the Hindoos would have refused thus to insult their dear Crishna. It is so sacred a river, that, formerly, no bridge was allowed to be built over it. The late Rajah was the first who suffered the bridge we had crossed to-day to be built. When it was finished, the Brahmins declared it would not stand; but they own that the good fortune of the British in India is too strong for Crishna Bye (the Lady Crishna) to oppose; or, as the little Brahmin children near it believe, because the spell was broken by burying a living Brahmin child under one of the foundations. [1]

[1] Throughout the whole length of its course in the Sattara territory, the Crishna is nowhere used for purposes of irrigation, except at one spot near Sattara, where a small patch of land is irrigated by four leathern buckets, which draw water from the sacred river. This land belonged to a very industrious gardener, a very pious votary of Crishna. One night, the river goddess appeared to him in a dream, and told him, as a reward for his piety and industry, she was pleased to allow him to set up a well of four buckets, and irrigate his land from the holy stream, which he did, and his descendants have continued to draw from the same stream to this day. Many others, the villagers say, have endeavoured to follow his example, but some evil always befals them; while the gardener's family have always prospered—

Towards evening we arrived at a river which was so swollen, it was impossible to cross it, and we passed the night by the side of the rapid, roaring stream. Early the next morning (the waters having subsided), we were able to continue our journey, and to reach Poona without any further disaster.

a sure proof, they say, that to him, and him alone, the goddess gave leave to use her stream. The irrigation in the neighbourhood all depends either on wells or on the small stream which fall into the Crishna.

CHAPTER III.

SHORTLY before we left India, the railroad at
Bombay was completed to a short distance beyond
Tannah.

This was the first railroad opened in India. It
can well be imagined what astonishment and excitement it caused among the natives, as well as what
surprise it occasioned to many Europeans; for there
were Anglo-Indians at Bombay, who had not been
in Europe for many years, and who, therefore, had
not seen a rail-road. The station from whence we
started on a kind of experimental trip, is at Byculla,
about three miles from the fort of Bombay.

A very handsome new temple had been com-menced before the railroad was contemplated, actually contiguous to the station, and was on the verge of completion when the latter was opened.

A railway station, and a Hindoo temple in juxta-position—the work of the rulers and the ruled. Could one possibly imagine buildings more opposite in their purposes, or more indicative of the charac-ter of the races? the last triumphs of science side by side with the superstitions of thousands of years ago.

We made the journey from the commencement to the end of the line, as far as it was finished.

As we approached Tannah, we saw, on the left, the ruins of a Portuguese church, where St. Francis Xavier is said to have performed a great miracle, that of converting a number of Pagans to Christianity at one time.[1]

When we reached Tannah, a place near the rail-road was shown us where a few months ago a tiger was shot. This reminds me of a drawing (I think it was in ' Punch') in which a tiger is represented

[1] In the Dictionnaire Historique, St. Francis Xavier is called " L'Apôtre des Indes," John, King of Portugal, sent him to the East Indies, in 1542.

carrying away a stoker, or a porter on an Indian railroad. However, I do not think this will ever happen, as the steam-engines will speedily drive away all the tigers and jackals from the islands of Bombay and Salsette.

A few miles from Tannah, we stopped to look at the scenery, which is very beautiful. We were protected from the sun by a very high hill about seven hundred feet high. On it had lived in peaceful retirement, a few months previously, numerous monkeys. They had been frightened away, and had sought some more secluded spot.

When I had last travelled on a railroad, (going to Southampton, *en route* to India), how different were the objects which had then presented themselves to those that I saw this afternoon. Here and there a religious mendicant standing with his eyes wide open, staring at the puffing, blowing engine, thinking it might be another avatar of Crishna!—a bullock gharee creeping on at about two miles an hour!—or a bridal-party on foot, the bride walking behind the bridegroom, the progress of the procession being momentarily arrested by the novelty of the sight. The scene was altogether curious, and very interesting.

The introduction of railways into India, must, in

time, destroy the influence of caste; the natives will be obliged to mix more with each other, and, by degrees, such distinctions will disappear. It is to be hoped so; for, so long as caste exists, it is to be feared, that even education will do but little to introduce Christianity in India. All those who become Christians are considered outcasts by those who still remain heathens; and are deserted even by relations; therefore, unless the individual be protected by those who have been instrumental in his conversion, he is without any means of getting a livelihood.

Not long ago, a wealthy Hindoo at Bombay wishing to go to Tannah by the railroad, expressed a desire that he might not be in the same carriage with natives of another caste from himself. He was told this could not be the case; he must travel with other passengers of the same class; he was obliged, of course, to submit.

As we rushed along, on our return to Parell, on the occasion of the excursion, of which I have spoken, the palms appeared more majestic than usual, and to look down upon us with contempt and disgust, while the monster of an engine sent forth an unearthly, protracted yell, as it tore over the flats of Bombay, where, after sunset, the jackals had for so long held undisputed sway.

The day for our leaving Bombay arrived at last; and, on the 29th of December, 1853, we embarked on board the *Feroze*—a ship I had christened three or four years before.

As we left the shore, the sun was just setting; Colaba, with its houses, palms, and lighthouse, stood out in deep shadow against a crimson sky, and I remained on deck till we had passed all the well-known scenery in the harbour, straining my eyes to catch the last glimpse of all my old haunts.

The confinement of a ship is never tedious to me, and in the little incidents that take place on board, and in the variety of character exhibited by my fellow-passengers, I always find constant amusement.

In some of the large American steamers there are, I believe, nurseries for the children, which are so placed in the ship that the little travellers cannot be troublesome to those on board who may dislike their companionship. In our steamer, the very young children began to cry at early dawn, while others of a larger growth would scream and romp all day on deck—as a matter-of-course, perpetually annoying some old bachelor who had a most particular aversion to their playful gambols.

Those only who have made long sea voyages can tell what the pleasure is when land is first sighted ; all run to the sides of the vessel, and—though, perhaps, no eyes but those of an experienced sailor can distinguish it—the very idea of land having been seen by anyone gives new life to all on board.

The weather was bright and beautiful; there were watery creatures, strange to look at, floating under and on the waves, and, as the sun shone on them, they looked like coloured gems; but still more beautiful were the effects caused on the sea, at night, by the phosphoric animalculæ.

There was a truly *English* marine band on board ; a more discordant one I never heard, and during many evenings we had to bear with, not listen to, that wretched bad music. It played, whenever dinner was announced, the 'Roast beef of old England;' of which it was cruel to be reminded, for we had nothing but the thin bad mutton (which recalled to my recollection "the affectionate Butcher,") and the tough fowls of Bombay.

As we approached Aden, after eight days' voyage from Bombay, every one looked brighter and more animated.

Aden is a strange place, but is grand in its scenery, with its bold, rugged rocks and sharp-peaked summits; all of a brownish, dingy-red colour, with scarcely a weed visible in the fissures in the rocks.

On approaching the harbour, the place lost somewhat of its sombre appearance. In the far distance faint outlines of mountains were seen. The bungalows of the Europeans, and the number of ships and boats on the dark-blue water, which dashed up against the gloomy, bleak rocks, gave a more cheerful appearance to this wild and dreary scenery.

But, if possible, far stranger and more wild are the Sumali natives of the north-western peninsula. They seem, indeed, inhabitants of another world; at all events, they scarcely look like human beings. They wear very little covering; their skins are of a dingy, burnt sienna colour. Their hair is naturally black, curly and woolly; but they have a custom of dying it a deep red. I saw one of these men, who had his head prepared for the process of dyeing. His hair was covered with a thick paste of shell-lime, so closely smeared all over his head that, to all appearance, he had on a skull-cap. When the paste becomes dry, it is removed; and the hair, being thus dyed, is greased with mutton fat, when the head much resembles a 'mop,' used by housemaids in England. Nothing can look more unearthly than these creatures, when their red hair, which usually curls close, becomes lank, and falls in wiry ringlets over their copper-coloured faces.

The hotel—or, more properly, the travellers' bungalow—at Aden is similar to the 'places of entertainment' one meets with in Western India, where people are made as uncomfortable as they can be—but with this addition that the cockroaches at Aden dispute with the traveller the possession of the skeleton bed which stands in the unfurnished room. This wretched hotel has received the name of the 'Hotel of the Prince of Wales.' It is a very long building, with broad verandahs. All the ladies and children who could not have separate rooms, occupied together a large apartment, furnished only with divans. Sleep was out of the question, for the dogs barked and howled all night.

The voyage up the Red Sea, from Aden to Suez, is full of interest. Towards the evening of the day we left the former place, we saw the African coast, and a few small islands, close to the larger Strait of Babel Mandel, well known as the 'Gate of Tears.'

The ranges of distant hills, and the imposing nearer mountains, with their peaked summits, render the scenery of this part of the Red Sea extremely grand. Several days intervened between our passing the smaller strait of Babel Mandel, and our arrival at Suez. The time, however, slipped pleasantly by. The day before we reached the port, the magnificent range of Mount Sinai was distinctly visible, and the position of Tor was pointed out to us.

Towards the evening of the last day's voyage, we passed, on our left, an opening in the mountains between Abu Deraj and Jebel Atakah——being the valley in which some of the learned of the present day agree that most probably the children of Israel encamped before they crossed the Red Sea. It was with feelings of intense interest that we looked at this valley, and, indeed, at the surrounding scenery, so full of biblical recollections.

Here, for the first time, we had a truly European sky—that well-known dull, heavy, grey sky, which seems to weigh on one's spirits, and I felt, I was no longer in ' the East.' Suez was soon in sight. As we approached, all forgot Moses, and Pharoah, Aaron and Miriam, and thought only of the necessities of the moment—all the passengers wishing to secure a few hours' rest before landing, which they did about two in the morning. There was no choice, for the conveyances of the Transit Company were waiting for them.

We, however, did not land till some hours after, and when I went on deck the ship looked quite deserted; all the cabin-doors were wide open—all the inmates gone! The berths containing no vestige of their late occupants—save a tin-jug and basin, nothing was left to tell the story! and persons who had been in constant companionship for nearly a fortnight would never, probably, meet again.

The carriage sent for us by the Pacha of Egypt, to convey us to Cairo, was a most comfortable coach, of Parisian manufacture, drawn by six animals, some of which were horses, others mules. They set off at great speed, which, however, did not last long, as the sand was occasionally too deep to proceed rapidly. Afterwards, however, whenever the road admitted of it, we were carried along at the rate of ten miles an hour. Our servants followed in a vehicle, very much like an omnibus, drawn by four horses.

A few miles to our right was the fort of Ajrud, where pilgrims receive shelter and protection. To our left, at the extremity of the

sandy plain over which we travelled, were high
hills; all, for miles around us, being nothing but
sandy desert. A few stunted acacia-bushes were
occasionally seen, their leaves covered with sand
and dust. Now and then, camels passed on, laden
with baggage, going to Suez; and, strewn about
in all directions, were skeletons of many of these
animals that, having become exhausted under their
burdens, had been left on the way to die, and
become the prey of vultures and other birds. Occasionally we saw some half-starved goats, standing
on their hind-legs, nibbling at the dusty leaves of
the stunted acacias.

Refreshments were provided at the stations in
the desert between Suez and Cairo. The rooms in
these stations are large, furnished with divans, and
the traveller finds the tables well covered with tur-
keys, fowls, and hams. Near one of the stations,
I think the middle one, Abbas Pacha had built
one of those enormous palaces which are so numerous in Egypt. There it stood, looking desolate—
a great staring building, with no tree, no bush
near it to soften the dreary solitude of the scene.
The furniture, I understand, came from England.

We reached Cairo at midnight, having been
about twelve hours on the road from Suez. It had

been a very hot day, and it would have been agreeable to have found 'à pied à terre' at the hotel to which we drove at that late hour. After the extremely hot day the night was chilly, and we felt painfully that we had left India, and that we should have no more tropical nights.

At Shepperd's Hotel we received the pleasing intelligence that there was not a room to be had. So away we drove to the Hotel d'Europe. "Is this the Hotel d'Europe?" was our anxious inquiry. "Yes," said a man, with a very gruff voice, evidently not in the best humour at having been roused from his slumbers. Following this sleepy personage, who had hurried on a loose kind of smock-frock, but whose legs and feet were bare, and who held a tallow candle in one hand, we were led through many dark passages, narrow, long, and by no means fragrant, till we came to a door, which it appeared impossible to open. After some little time, however, we gained admittance to a room, most cold and gloomy in appearance; here the smock-frocked gentleman put his candle on the table, and left us to seek the master of the house, who at last came. He was a fat, portly gentleman, and stalked about in a pompous manner, giving us at first but little hope of anything more than one room for seven people! After some reflection, however, he found accommodation for our rather large party, and in due course of time all was quiet, and we retired to rest.

CHAPTER IV.

CAIRO—FIRST VIEW AT CAIRO—SCENE FROM THE HOTEL—TRA-
VELLERS AND DONKEY BOYS — MATAREEH-HELIOPOLIS, THE
ANCIENT ON—PALACES AT CAIRO—VIEW FROM THE CITADEL—
DINNER AT A COPT'S HOUSE — BAZAAR — MOSQUES—SHOOBRA—
TOMBS OF THE CALIPHS—VISIT OF AN ARMENIAN LADY—
PETRIFIED FOREST.

THERE are, no doubt, many persons who, when young, or even when, like myself, they are no longer so, have felt, on arriving at a strange place, late at night, an impatient longing for morning, from a wish to see the view from their windows; and this wish I scarcely ever remember to have felt more strongly than I did on reaching Cairo—a town I had long been desirous to visit, and which I knew to be unlike any other, Lane's charming book— 'The Modern Egyptians'—being fresh in my mind.

At early dawn, I looked on a very narrow street.
Directly opposite was a small, mysterious-looking
latticed window in a white wall, behind which
rose a graceful minaret, and a few date-palms, which
I was glad to see, for they reminded me of the
lovely island of Bombay. To the right was a good-
sized house, with a large and very handsome projecting window of the kind so common in this most
picturesque and Arabian-night-like of cities. In
the vicinity were many smaller windows, the blinds
of which were drawn down. For a short time, all
was quiet; presently, a man passed carrying a
large pewter can, the contents of which looked like
milk, cream, or curds. He commenced making
known with a loud voice to the neighbourhood
what he had to sell, and his cry aroused the slum-
bering inhabitants to the occupations of daily life
in Cairo. From the balcony of the hotel, situated
in that part of Cairo called the ' Uzbekeeh,' I enjoyed a variety of amusing scenes; and, although I
passed some time in the place, every hour almost
brought something fresh, entertaining, and worthy
of observation.

This morning, an old man walked into my sitting-
room, with a long cloak descending to his feet, and
with his hat on, holding in his hand a bunch of

ostrich plumes. I thought he was mad at first, till I discovered he was desirous of selling these feathers. Not finding a purchaser, however, he quickly retreated, and I saw him riding away on a donkey at full gallop, a boy running after him with a box of ostrich feathers in his arms!

Opposite the hotel were a few fine acacias, under which generally stood several donkeys and their attendant boys,[1] anxiously waiting to be hired.

[1] Groups of these boys are always seen near hotels in Cairo. They are, in fact, the 'cads' of the place. But woe betide the hapless traveller just arrived from England, and not aware of the strange uncouth proceedings of these urchins. Anxious to ride and see the city, he beckons to one, and in a moment he finds himself surrounded by a dozen, and their donkeys; each screaming out the merits both of his animal and himself. Almost all of them now know a few words of English. 'Dat, sir, bad donkey.' 'Dis no kick, sir.' In the meantime, they are fighting with each other for the poor stranger's patronage; all close in—the tumult becomes general; while the unfortunate cause of the dispute is scarcely visible in the crowd around him; an uplifted arm, and every now and then angry language, showing, however, that life is not quite extinct. When, at length, he has selected, and is in the act of putting one leg over a donkey, he finds his leg seized; and he is pulled roughly by the arm, and dragged towards a different beast. At last, with his coat nearly torn off his back, he succeeds in securing a 'monture,' and away he gallops, glad to escape with his life. I often witnessed such scenes as this from the window of the hotel, and they never failed to amuse me. It should, however, be borne in mind that it is far better to ride than drive through the bazaars.

Under the trees were also sellers of sugar-cane, and female orange merchants. These women wear the 'burko,' or face-veil, which leaves the eyes only visible. Sometimes, a donkey passed, laden with pig-skins full of water, or with heavy bundles of grass; then Copt priests, in black robes; and, occasionally, an Egyptian dame riding (as Egyptian dames do ride) *en cavalier*, her ample black cloak floating in the wind, and looking like a large balloon —her full silk trousers, tied tight round the ancle, terminated by a pair of French grey cloth 'brodequins,' tipped with polished leather; while another, perhaps immediately following her, would have on the usual yellow morocco boots, formerly universally worn by ladies in Cairo. From time to time, a body of the Pacha's troops would file by, or a European carriage, full of strangers, *lionizing*, be rapidly driven past; then all would be concealed by a cloud of Cairo dust, which, enveloping at once ladies, soldiers, quadrupeds, and crowd, rendered my hasty retreat from the balcony necessary.

One morning, very early, we left Cairo to visit Matareeh and Heliopolis, the On [1] of Scripture.

---

[1] "And Pharaoh called Joseph's name Zaphnath-paaneah, and he gave him to wife Asenath, the daughter of Potipherah, Priest of On."—Genesis xli. 45.

The coachman took us a wrong way, and, in about an hour after starting, we found there was no longer any carriage-road; we, therefore, determined to walk over the fields, and send the carriage round to meet us. We hesitated, indeed, at first, fearing the power of the sun; but, recollecting we were no longer in the tropics, boldly pursued our excursion on foot. None but those who have passed some time in India can understand the sense of enjoyment felt on the occasion of a 'first walk' in Egypt at mid-day in January (when the sun, though powerful, is in no degree prejudicial); or the feeling of re-covered liberty, which, on first arriving at Cairo, has so great a charm for those who have been long accustomed to take the air only at stated hours in the morning and evening.

We found Matareeh a miserable village. In a pretty garden there stands the tree under which, it is said, our Lord, with the Virgin Mary and Joseph, rested on their coming into Egypt. This tree is a sycamore, very like the large Indian wild fig-tree.

It is a pity to throw a doubt on an old tradition, but there is nothing in this fine old tree to make one believe it is eighteen hundred years old. Its trunk and boughs have been disfigured by travellers, who have thought to immortalize themselves by cutting their names in the bark.

We rested some time in the garden, and I thought of what a foreigner had said to me a few days previously, when speaking of this place. He exclaimed—" *One can well e-mar-gene Josef telling his loaf dere to Asenate.*"

There is nothing remaining of On, or Heliopolis, but low mounds, which surround a space of about one mile in length, and half a mile in breadth, and one obelisk of red granite about sixty-two feet in height. This obelisk stands in a pool of water, surrounded by willows and a few firs. It bears the name of Osistasen the First, in whose reign Sir Gardner Wilkinson supposes Joseph arrived in Egypt.

Heliopolis signifies ' the city of the sun ;' and here stood the famous Bethshemeth—' the house of the sun'—the image of which Jeremiah, in his prophecies, foretold Nebuchadnezzar would break, and further, that he would burn the houses of the gods of the Egyptians with fire.

A month's residence in Cairo is not too long ; there is so much to see in the city and its environs. One could see all in a much shorter space of time, but it would be a very hasty and unsatisfactory survey; and I do not think that even a month would afford time for an excursion to any of the pyramids.

There are several palaces at Cairo, of which, however, the exteriors are not at all handsome. They are almost all very large, but really not worth seeing; few are in good order. There is a small one, built by Mahomet Ali, with a very small garden attached to it. From the windows of this house we had a view of the Nile, the city, and the pyramids, which are about twelve miles distant. With the exception of marble floors, and cashmere coverings for the divans in the principal apartments, there is nothing handsome. All the palaces have large, lofty, and well-proportioned rooms, all hung with rich silk curtains; but there is a sad mixture of splendour and bad taste, although the furniture is from Paris. The wainscoting is sometimes stained to look like marble.

In one palace, lately built, there was in one room a beautiful large fountain, the ornaments of which were finely and sharply carved. Suite after suite of rooms did I traverse in those royal residences, and I came away with a confused recollection of divans, chairs covered with a rich brocaded silk, heavy gilt-tables, gaudy carpets, huge modern French vases, full of artificial flowers, large gilt porcelain clocks, and glass chandeliers—not a picture—not a book—to rest your eyes on, to relieve them from the mass of glittering, glaring objects in these numerous saloons. What a relief it was to leave them, and to gaze awhile on a minaret, however ruinous it might be, or a mosque, with its graceful arches and richly-ornamented porch; even a *tumble-down* wall was an agreeable object to the eye, after so much gorgeous finery.

One day that I went to see the view from the citadel, I was accompanied by a lady, who had passed many years at Cairo; and although the city and its neighbourhood were quite familiar to her, she was as enthusiastic with regard to the history of Egypt, as if she had only arrived there a few days before.

On the other side of the Nile, or as it is called in Scripture the 'river of Egypt,' stand at this day the three pyramids, which existed even before the arrival of Abraham, which were witnesses of the miracles of Moses, and were there when the water in the land was turned into blood, when the 'thick darkness covered all the land of Egypt three days,' and when the most dreadful of all the twelve plagues, that of the death of the first-born, 'from the first-born of Pharaoh that sat on the throne, down even unto the first-born of the maid-servant that was behind the mill,' visited that king and his people.

How many are the important events which the view from the citadel recalls to the mind! It is, in fact, a chart of sacred and profane history spread out before one—when looking down on this curious and extensive landscape (for I cannot call it beautiful, though here and there, there are some beautiful objects) all the various actors on the striking scene were present to the memory. The interesting history of Joseph was brought vividly before one, and the arrival of his family, and residence in Goshen, which is generally believed to have been in the district around Heliopolis.

Beyond the Nile is the site of Memphis. And as we gaze, the invasions of Nebuchadnezzar, and of Cambyses, of Alexander the Great, the acts of Antony and Cleopatra, and of Cæsar Augustus rush into the recollection; next follows the history of Egypt as a Roman province, its seizure by Amer in the reign of Caliph Omar, in 622,[1] and its conquest by the Turks in 1517—while a glance in the direc-

[1] According to Sir Gardner Wilkinson.

tion of the residence (in the Frank quarter) occupied by Napoleon Bonaparte brings us down to the invasion of the French, and the battle of the Pyramids.

A Copt family having invited a small party of English (amongst whom I was fortunately included) to dinner, we went early in the afternoon to the house of our entertainer, the invitation having been given in the name of the master of the family. He was wealthy, and belonged to the middle class of citizens at Cairo. Ascending a very dark staircase we reached a landing, near which was the kitchen. It was full of women evidently busy preparing for the approaching feast. We then entered a sitting-room in that part of the house called the Hareem. This room was very 'Europeanized.' There was the divan always found in Egyptain houses, but all else was *un-eastern*, and among other things was a modern French gilt clock, which somehow did not look in character with the Copt's apartment.

The seat of honour in Egypt is at the angle of the divan, and there the ' burrah bibbee' was led by the host ; she climbed somewhat ungracefully thereon, for the divans are usually rather high from the ground.

After we were all seated, and the host had placed himself opposite us on a chair, the conversation became very animated between him and one of our party, who spoke Arabic very well. In a few minutes the lady of the house came in, salutations passed, and having received permission from her husband, she sat down on a chair by his side. She had on a winter dress. The full trowsers were of fine grey cloth, as was also the long vestment, called ' yelek,' which fits tight to the body, and is of such a length as to completely cover the feet. A small shawl was twisted round the waist. Over the yelek was the long open robe called ' gibbeh,' of purple cloth, richly embroidered in gold ; this dress was even longer than the yelek ; a veil of black net hung down from behind her red cap, as also the ' safa '—the Egyptian head-dress made of black silk cords covered with small gold coins—it is the same head-dress that is always seen on the statues of Isis. The lady's hair in front was cut short round her forehead, but fell in plaits and tresses down her shoulders ; and a bandeau of inferior diamonds ornamented the cap, or taboosh. While we were talking, pipes and coffee were brought in ; the mother, wife, and daughter of the host walked in and out of the room from time to time ; this, however, they did not do nimbly, as the long ' gibbeh,' covering their feet, prevented rapid movement, and their dresses were heavy from the gold embroidery with which they were adorned. The daughter was very young, and rather pretty.

After some time, dinner was announced. The gentleman said he had prepared the repast as well as he could according to European custom, adding, that his country's customs were so barbarous.

We, however, preferred a dinner à l'Egyptienne, but kept our napkins, which was lucky, as I had previously had but a faint idea of the proceedings at a dinner completely eastern in all its forms and ways.

The ladies of the house did not sit at table with the host and his guests, but continued walking to and from the kitchen with the black woman slaves who brought in the numerous dishes; these were placed on the table by the old mother of the host. The wife walked about in a stately manner.

When the attack on the viands began, how glad I was the napkins had been retained! There were altogether, during the dinner, about fifty dishes. The first thing that appeared was a large tureen of vermicelli soup, into which we all plunged our spoons. After this we helped ourselves, with our fingers, to whatever pleased our fancy; and the gentleman occasionally offered with his fingers, dainty bits from his own plate to his guests, with which they all were obliged to appear perfectly delighted. Dish after dish was put on, and then removed from the table. At last, the good mother appeared, holding a plate, on which was a large joint of lamb. She put it on the table, bent over it, and tore it open with her two hands!—displaying, with some pride, the interior, which consisted of raisins, rice, chestnuts, and other fruits. She then presented each person with a large piece of meat, her hands being thrust into the dish and withdrawn laden with all kinds of savoury condiments, which she heaped up on our plates. The lady of highest rank, 1 remarked, had Benjamin's portion. Then the kind old dame trotted off, her hands shining with grease, to bring other dishes— never reflecting what an advantage it would be if she washed her fingers in the interim; but she probably thought this would be a useless operation, as it would have to be so often repeated. Our bread was a large, flat, round cake, about the size of a plate; and each person had a tumbler of the red wine of the country, very sour, and much like that drank by the peasants in the south of France. During dinner, the servants not employed, were outside the house, welcoming us with a singular cry. It was one of joy, and is called the 'Zekka-rite.' This is a custom when people entertain their friends.

As soon as the meat courses had disappeared, a great variety of sweetmeats were offered to us; one dainty after another being pressed on us; and when we had left the table, the ladies of the house pursued me with bits of oranges and bananas till I at last escaped to the black slaves, who were waiting with water and soap for our hands, over which the water from the ewer was poured by one of the attendants, and it may be well imagined these ablutions were not only pleasant but necessary.

I wish I could have procured a bill of fare, but I remember several dishes. There were stewed pigeons, chickens, and a pillau of lamb, minced meat and tomatas, cauliflower dressed with vinegar, balls of fried meat, rice in gravy and in milk, syrup of pears and bananas in large glass bowls, biscuits and cakes of flour and butter, sugared over.

We returned to the sitting-room, where pipes and coffee awaited us. In the meantime, the ladies of the family and their friends had fallen on the mangled remains of the feast, and their loud talking and merry voices proclaimed them very happy.

The gentleman called to them very often, but they all turned a deaf ear, thinking no doubt it was their turn to be joyous, so he went himself, and the sherbet was brought, which we conceived *must* be the end of the festivities, and rose to go, after all kinds of compliments and pretty speeches to our host.

As we passed the banqueting-room, we stopped to say farewell to the ladies, and to thank them, through our interpreter, for their hospitality; but had I understood their language, I should not have known what they replied, for they all ran, with many of their friends (women, of course), to the door, and all spoke at the same time and with their mouths full.

The bazaars at Cairo are, indeed, a scene of animation and bustle; one meets crowds of people. On each side of the narrow street, barely wide enough in some instances to admit a single carriage, are small shops, the retail merchants sitting in a recess, and on a raised platform about three feet higher than the street. This recess is so small, that scarcely more than two persons at a time can enter to make purchases, so that customers generally stand outside the small shops, which are quite open, and converse with the seller, who sits on his raised seat, usually smoking a pipe, and appearing to care very little whether people buy or not. The crowd is often very dense, and if you stop as you pass to look at the number of shops, you are quite bewildered. There are muslin kerchiefs, and slippers, and bags embroidered in gold; silk, lace, and tabooshes, rich silks, and shawls, ostrich feathers from Abyssinia, woollen cloths from Europe, pipes and slippers from Constantinople, embroidered silks from Damascus, prayer-carpets, bornooses ; besides firearms, tobacco, coffee, and spices of all sorts. The shops where sweetmeats are sold are exceedingly numerous. Among the ' bon-bons,'—if I may so call them—I remarked ships, birds, and figures of men, all of sugar, and of a rose-colour.

We stopped sometimes at a jeweller's and admired a pretty coffee-service of silver or gold filagree work, or sundry female ornaments ; some of which are of beautiful forms.

Then we passed on to other shops; and what a variety of persons did we meet! First, perhaps, a reputed saint, dressed in a coat of patches of different colours, asking for alms. Then several young cadets, just arrived at Cairo on their way to India, full of life and spirits, with young and fresh minds, enjoying the curious scene : some of them, alas ! may never come back, or if they do return after many long years, may do so with bodily and mental vigour alike impaired by a long sojourn under a tropical sun ;[1] a sad reflection to intrude itself amidst the lively doings around us in the bazaars ; but such gloomy thoughts

[1] "Since the above remark was written, my melancholy presentiment has been but too fatally fulfilled in the case of many young officers who lost their lives in the late horrible mutiny."

are dissipated by the somewhat too close vicinity of a Bedouin Arab mounted on a camel, who seems to think all should make way for him, as in reality all do, to avoid the certainty of being knocked down or crushed. European ladies in flounced muslins, with very unveiled faces, and wearing the little bonnet which just covers the back of the head, then ride by, mingled with Turkish matrons, the persons of the latter being nearly concealed by their black cloaks; Copts, known by their dark turbans; sellers of vegetables, fruit, and sweatmeats, water carriers, men selling sherbet in tin jugs, carriages, and horsemen, press on the numerous crowd on foot, and it seems marvellous that the latter are not trodden underfoot by the camels, or by the horses, crushed among the carriages, or pushed down by the donkeys.

It is impossible to note all one sees in the streets and bazaars of this city, or to become acquainted with all the scenes of every-day life, during a short stay in the country, so one leaves it after all with a very imperfect idea of the manners and customs of the inhabitants. On one occasion, on our return from the bazaars, we met a funeral procession; the bier was carried by men, preceded by others chanting in a very slow melancholy tone. Female mourners followed, and I remarked blue strips of linen tied round their heads, the ends hanging down. These were the relations and domestic servants of the deceased. Lane mentions, that in the funeral scenes represented on the walls of ancient Egyptian tombs, we often see females with a similar bandage round their heads. The women were wailing and crying, and nearly overpowered the voices of the men who were chanting. In a crowded street I could observe but little of this funeral procession, but the burial rites are fully described by Lane, who enters into all the curious particulars attending them.

The mosques are very numerous at Cairo. We went to see the new one, which is not yet finished, begun by Mahomet Ali. At first it was difficult to gain admittance, as I had no slippers; but the heart of one of the prophet's followers, who stood at the entrance of the mosque, was softened towards me, and he said he would send for two handkerchiefs to wrap round my feet; which, being procured, I was allowed to go into the mosque, the large court of which is very handsome, as is also the fountain for ablution. The pillars in the mosque are of marble, and in the dome there are stained windows; the wood of the pulpit, and of the staircase leading to it, is painted green, and gilt, the effect of which is very tawdry, and unsatisfactory. It is almost always the case with handsome buildings in the east, and I found it so here, that nothing is in harmony; near the fine marble pillars were suspended lanterns of the commonest kind; but it is altogether a beautiful mosque. It is as well, however, to see this mosque before the others in Cairo, for they and their minarets, although in a ruinous state, must delight every admirer of architecture. I visited many; but those known as the Tayloon, the Kalaoon, the Hassanin, El Hakem, El Ghoree, and Hassan, pleased me the most. All the ornaments in these buildings deserve a minute inspection; but there is scarcely time or opportunity for this, as the crowds of curious persons, both inside and outside the mosque, press on strangers, and it is impossible to inspect the buildings with any comfort; still, I had time to admire many a window adorned with graceful tracery, grand porches ornamented with beautiful cornices, lofty columns, and elegant minarets.

We did not fail to visit the well, known as Joseph's Well, called so from the Caliph Yoosef, though it is generally believed to have been hewn in the rock by the ancient Egyptians. A

lady who visited this well, remarked she supposed
it must be the pit into which Joseph was cast by
his brethren !

Our janissary, Abousaid, pointing out to us the
residences of the members of Abbas Pacha's
family, remarked, that " many wives here not
good. English custom to have one wife very good
—very good," he kept saying, as he rode on before
us, whirling his silver stick in the air. It seemed
to me the poor janissary might be unfortunate in
his domestic arrangements, and that he had found
some trouble and inconvenience in having more
than one wife.

Among the various objects to be visited in the
neighbourhood of Cairo, is Shoobra, a residence of
one of the princes of the pacha's family. As we
left the town to go there, we crossed the railroad,
which is to unite Alexandria and Cairo. The road
to Shoobra is shaded on both sides by acacias and
large sycamore-trees, and runs frequently close to
the Nile, across which the three pyramids of
Geezeh are distinctly visible. We did not enter
the palace, some of the ladies of the family of the
prince being there. The gardens are large, and
prettily laid out; European, as well as tropical
flowers being cultivated there. The English stock

in these gardens was very fragrant, and it grew beside the lovely Bengal gold-mohr, which, however, has nothing to boast of but its brilliant beauty.

There is a fantastic summer-house, or kiosk, in the gardens, the windows of which are prettily painted, and a handsome metal chandelier is suspended from the ceiling. There is, also, a very large building, with a spacious corridor, surrounding an extensive marble bath. Heathen deities are painted, (by Italian artists) on the ceilings of these corridors: there is, also, a portrait of Mahomet Ali, and on each side of him pictures of the Virgin, with drapery round her head, a wreath of flowers in one hand, and a staff in the other.

An Egyptian, showing these pictures to a lady, said—" That is Joseph's wife, whom you Christians worship."

At the four corners of the corridors are small but handsome chambers, which contain many pretty things; large silver palm-trees, about five feet high, standing on handsome tables; beautiful cabinets; curious chandeliers, with drops of different-coloured glass, looking like emeralds, sapphires, amethysts, &c.

Before we left this place, we went to see a lion

—a live one, not worth seeing—and a fine grand
St. Bernard dog, who was well worthy of a visit.

Among the many tombs most worthy of notice
in the vicinity of Cairo, are those usually called
the 'tombs of the Caliphs,' by Europeans. They
are outside the town, and stand in the arid, dusty
desert. Mosques are attached to the principal
ones, and it is sad to see these beautiful buildings
falling rapidly to decay. Many poor families live in
them, and children run out, asking strangers who
visit them for 'backshish,' but are soon put to
flight by the janissary with one twirl of his stick.

We were much struck by the beauty and ele-
gance of the architecture of these mosques, more
especially of that of El Ashraf Aboo-l Nusr
Kaedbai e'Zaheree, who died in 1496 A.D.

An Armenian lady whom I had visited, came to
return the compliment a few days afterwards.
Although a Christian, she retained, even when in
private, some part of the costume of the country,
and when she went out, dressed completely like an
Egyptian.

On arriving at my hotel, she even wore the face
veil, as also that very ungraceful covering, called
" Habarah." As soon as she entered the room,
however, she began to " *un-peel*," and this process

ended, appeared in a half-European, half-Egyptian dress. The conversation was confined to the state of her health and mine, and to the weather.

I told her that in England we had usually fine weather in the summer, and that the winters were severe; that in Egypt we found the winters beautiful, but had heard that the summers were very trying from the excessive heat, and clouds of dust, upon which she remarked, "Thus God alternately dispenses His blessings to all."

After rather a lengthened visit, she rose to go, and enveloped herself in garment after garment, till she became utterly shapeless, her eyes peering over the long 'burko' which descends to the feet. I watched her from the balcony, and the last glimpse I had of my friend was when she was mounting her donkey, which was caparisoned as it would be for a man.

One day we went to see the petrified forest. It is about six miles from the town. We drove some way over the sandy plain, passing many tombs, mosques, great mounds of earth, and limestone rocks, which, in the glare of a brilliant sunshiny day, were very distressing to the eyes. We went as far as the road would admit in a carriage, then rode on donkeys to what is called the petrified forest. It was a long ride, and the sand very deep. I thought we should nveer arrive ; the sand became deeper and deeper, and the poor donkey's legs quite sunk into it.

"How far ?" I asked· the donkey boy.

"Two minute."

On we went, the 'two minute,' and some more gone by, I asked again, "How far to the trees ?"

"Two minute," was the reply.

At last we reached what is called the petrified forest, which does not deserve the name, though there were many petrified trunks and boughs of trees of all sizes strewn about on the sand. Getting off our donkeys we sat some time on the ground gazing on the singular and desolate scene around.

A very high hill behind the citadel shut out all view to the left ; and around was sandy desert, not a tree visible. Far away, the tops of two or three minarets rose over a sandy mound ; and dotted about the desert, were camels plodding along under their Arab riders.

As we returned to the town, we rode to a ravine, into which a spring of water flows from the hills, it is called 'Moses' Well.' In the rocky fissures

this ravine, grew a hanging shrub, the only
sh or green thing we had seen during our
cursion, except the small flowering weeds that
ionally peeped out among the stones and sand.

CHAPTER V.

CAIRO—ENGLISH CEMETERY—OLD CAIRO—VISIT TO A PERSIAN
LADY—ISLE OF RODA—NILOMETER—GIRLS' SCHOOL—THE DER-
VISHES—VISIT TO A TURKISH LADY—"YOUNG EGYPT"—PYRA-
MIDS OF GEEZAH—THE SPHINX—MEMPHIS—EXCAVATIONS AT
SAKKARAA.

ONE day we went to the English cemetery, on the
way to Old Cairo. The wind was high and cold,
the sun scorching: it was almost the sun of the
tropics, with the searching east wind of England;
and to complete the '*agrémens*' of the ride, the
dust rose up in clouds, nearly blinding and choking
us; but, as our time in Egypt was limited, we did
not mind the wind and weather, but persevered in
our excursion.

The cemetery is surrounded by walls, and is
laid out in walks, and trees and flowers have
been planted in vain to make this melancholy
place look less dismal. On one side of the garden

are buried those who had arrived ill from India, having remained, as is often the case, alas! too long in that country.

We sauntered round the inclosure, then mounted our donkeys and proceeded to Old Cairo (originally named Forstat, which signifies leather-tent, as Amer, who conquered Egypt in the Caliphate of Omar, A.D. 622, is said to have pitched his tent here when he besieged the Romans in their fortress). There are vast mounds of earth, showing the city to have been at one time considerable in extent. The old Roman fortress contains a singular medley of buildings—Coptic and Greek churches; convents occupied by Armenians, Syrians, and Copts; the ruins of a temple dedicated to Diana; a synagogue; and a village of Christians—all closely crowded together in a confused mass, with narrow paths and lanes leading from one part to another. The wretchedness of the habitations of the inmates of what was once the Roman camp is lamentable. Here is to be found true Egyptian dirt; but there is so much to see, I very soon forgot it, climbing staircase after staircase most perseveringly, to visit the various objects; among them the Coptic churches, which, though dirty and much decayed, interested me deeply. The ceiling of one was of gopher wood; and the church was divided into five compartments, separated by carved screens. On entering the church, we saw two baths for baptism—one for children, the other for adults. To the right was a part screened off, where the women remain during the service. A wooden screen always separates the 'heykel,' or chancel, from the rest of the church; before the entrance to the 'heykel' hangs a curtain. The panels of the screen were quaintly carved with scriptural subjects and crosses inlaid with mother-of-pearl. On the walls, near the chancel, were hung very ancient pictures of our Saviour, the Virgin Mary, and of various saints.

In one church, I saw the remains of several stone Corinthian pillars, which supported some part of the building, their capitals stuck in the ground!

There are no seats, the men rest themselves on crutches, for the services are long.

Under one church is the cave, or dungeon, where it is said the Holy Family took refuge when they reached Egypt. With lights, and preceded by a Copt priest, we descended a flight of steps, to what is now a little Coptic chapel. One can scarcely think our Lord would have been carried into a Roman fortress, when we know the family fled from the persecution of a Roman government; but it is

a pity to disturb this old story, so we will let it
pass.

The cave has, at all events, been regarded by
Christians of all denominations for ages as a very
sacred spot; and here those who are considered by
the *enlightened* world as superstitious, fanatics,
or bigots, come every year to perform their devotions. This little chapel is dark, and our tapers
barely rendered it visible, while the Copt priest, all
in black, held up his candle to shew us the corners,
ceilings, and altar, which is of stone; behind it is
a recess in the wall, where tradition says the
Saviour and His mother were concealed. In this
recess, is a Greek cross, deeply engraven; and on
the wall I observed a very old painting, nearly obliterated, but I could trace the form of a pyramid.
There is a font and a place for making the bread
for the holy Communion, which I also remarked in
the other churches here.

I had time to make a sketch of this interesting
little place, while the patient, good-natured priest,
stood near the altar throwing all the light upon it,
he himself being in the deepest possible shadow.

We were obliged to hurry on to the Coptic convent—a wretched place. One sister only appeared.
She rose up, coming out of a kind of den—not cell

—covered from head to foot with a large black
cloak. She showed us a chapel; ancient, but in a
ruinous state. She knew there was nothing more
to see, so she crawled back into a dark place from
whence she had emerged—(I think, much against her
will)—and she no doubt wondered what could have
brought us thither!

Time was passing quickly, so we hurried on to
the temple of Diana, a few pillars of which only
remain; and thence to the Greek church. What a
contrast was here! We had come from dilapidated
churches, from dirty streets had ascended staircase after staircase of broken steps; but now we
found ourselves in a church kept in the most
perfect order, and the delicious odour of incense
pervading the holy place.

It was, like all Greek churches, adorned with
endless paintings of St. George, many of our
Saviour, and the Virgin; some with silver plates
nailed round their heads, meant to represent
glories. In a vestibule outside the church there
was a truly melancholy sight. A harmless maniac
had been brought there, and was desired to look
on the picture of a certain saint suspended against
the wall, in hopes that his reason would return.
He was well dressed, very calm, but seemed to fix

his eyes on the ground, not on the picture; though he occasionally turned them towards us with a dull, despairing look, as if he thought his coming there would not be of that service to him which his friends deemed it might.

The last place we visited at Old Cairo was a chamber over an old gateway, where we saw a very ancient Christian record of the time of Diocletian. It is sculptured on wood. Among the figures represented, are those of the twelve apostles, who are marching in procession, and the Deity sitting on a globe, on each side of Him two winged angels, reminding one of the winged globe of the Egyptians. There is also an inscription in Greek.

The mosque of Amer at Old Cairo is in a ruinous state. There is a belief current among the Moslems in Egypt that, should this particular mosque fall into complete ruin, the Mahomedan power in the country would cease; therefore, every year, trifling repairs take place—but so trifling, that, to all appearance, no real good is done. There are two pillars near the door of the mosque to the south, about ten inches apart; between which pillars, it is asserted, none but those who believe in the prophet can succeed in passing.

The Copts, of whom I had seen and heard much since my stay in Egypt, interested me exceedingly. They certainly do not bear a high character; but may not their faults arise from the system of persecution under which they have suffered, more or less, from the time that Egypt was conquered by the Arabs to the present time? for they are still a marked people, being obliged to wear either a black or dark-blue turban. They are the undoubted descendants of the ancient Egyptians, deriving their name from Coptos, formerly a large city in Upper Egypt, now called Guft. The Coptic language, though not entirely lost, is almost a dead language. It is merely used in their liturgy, and other religious books.

The tyranny to which these poor people have been subjected by strangers, reminds one of the similar fate of the Jews—the prophecies regarding them being nearly as forcible as those relating to the latter people. "And the Egyptians will I give over into the band of a cruel Lord; and a fierce king shall rule over them, saith the Lord, the Lord of Hosts."—Isaiah xix. 4.

I was obliged to leave this most attractive place, "Old Musr," as it is sometimes called, and to return to keep an engagement at Cairo, having promised to visit a Persian lady, who had lately arrived. She had travelled from Persia with her attendants, under the protection of a Sheikh, who remained still in her house at Cairo.[1] An Armenian gentleman accompanied me, having very kindly offered himself as my interpreter.

We rode off on our donkeys at a lively pace to the Turkish quarter. In passing through the streets I heard some people at the door of a house half-singing, half-talking, while occasionally they struck bits of brass together; on inquiry, I heard they were reciting stories out of the Old Testament. How this reminded me of the kutha I used to hear at Poona, when the people related the deeds of their gods, occasionally beating metal instruments, which sounded like bells.

The palace in which the lady I was about to visit lived, had belonged to Ibrahim Pacha. It is a handsome one, ' triste,' however; but far preferable, even in its unfurnished, sombre state, to the glaring, showy modern palaces of the present princes of Egypt.

We entered the court-yard; projecting latticed windows of the second story overlooked the court;

[1] The lady was connected with the royal family of Persia, and had come to Cairo on ' urgent private affairs.'

and there were one or two rooms on the ground
floor, paved with white and black marble, arranged
in pretty patterns; the ceilings painted red and
green, and slightly gilt.

The first individual I saw was a black slave,
with the features of a Nubian, who I found was
the page, or 'groom of the chambers,' of the lady.
Round his head was a dirty handkerchief, the ends
hanging down behind; this was kept on by one
still more dirty, that, after passing under his chin,
was tied in a bow on the top of his head.   On his
tall, thin body, he wore a long Damascus silk robe,
the colours of which were nearly extinct; and his
emaciated legs were covered with stockings, which,
perhaps once white, were now iron-grey.   He led
us up a narrow stone staircase, the ceiling of which
was adorned with carvings of white marble.   At
last, after mounting a still narrower staircase, we
came to a vestibule.

The Bedouin sheikh, who had protected the lady
in her journey from Persia, met us with a rosary
in his hand.   He was dressed in the usual Bedouin
dress—the long brown robe, red-and-yellow handkerchief on his head, round which were twisted
cords made of camels' hair.   He was a tall, fine-
looking man, very grave, and rather pompous.

Following this evidently important personage, we entered a very large, unfurnished room, and found the lady standing on a raised platform, about two to three feet above the floor, and close to a large latticed window. There she stood, motionless, covered from head to foot with drapery, like the Hindoo saree. After mutual salutations, she begged me to sit down. Two small carpets and pillows were the only furniture of this elevated place, on which the lady and I were seated. Meanwhile, the Armenian gentleman and the sheikh had sat down on the ground a little behind the lady, as Persian ladies do not show their faces to strange men.

As soon as she was assured that I alone could see her, she opened by degrees the veil which concealed her features. First one eye peeped out, than the other, then the nose, till at last her whole figure and dress were completely visible. A lively dialogue then commenced between us, the interpreter sitting a little behind the lady, and with his face turned from her. She was not young, but had still, '*des prétensions.*' She had once been very pretty, and her expression was pleasing, with an arch, '*espiègle*' look, and her countenance lighted up most agreeably when she entered into conversation. She was very anxious to know who and what I was, where I came from, and where I could be going to; expressed surprise I did not go home to England, and asked why I travelled? To my answer, that I wished to see other countries and people, she said, it was strange if I could stay at home that I did not do so.

While we were talking and wondering at each other, she no doubt pitying my wandering unquiet spirit, and I her truly Eastern apathy and love of repose, I examined (woman-like) her dress, which was becoming as well as pretty. The vest was of cashmere—the sleeves were of different patterns, which had a curious effect; at the wrists were snow-white frilled cuffs, and gold buttons attached to the sleeves of the vest. The petticoat was of lilac silk. Over the head was a white linen veil which hung down on each side, nearly concealing her hair, which was jet black and glossy. I regret, however, to finish the account with adding, that she had a pair of large, bony, ill-shaped hands. Of course pipes were introduced, but I was not such an adept as my hostess in this accomplishment, and did little else but admire the ornamental part of the pipe, which was beautifully enamelled. Then appeared again that wretched

black slave, with a small tray and coffee, and I
thought it time to take leave. I therefore hinted to
the Armenian gentleman my wish to go away, but he
merely said, "Are you in a great hurry? Visits
like these last till sunset!" and as he quietly
resumed his pipe and entered again into conversation in a low voice with the Bedouin, I thought the
only thing I had to do was to resign myself to my
fate. In a few minutes sherbet was handed to us.
Then more talk followed, and my new acquaintance
regretted much I was about to leave Cairo, as I
should no doubt have passed a day with her, and
she one with me. She stretched her hospitality so
far as to beg me to remain at her house that night!
Presently, to my astonishment, in walked the black
slave again, carrying an entire tea equipage, which
he placed on the ground at the feet of the Bedouin
and the Armenian. The former while holding fast
his beads in one hand poured out the tea with the
other. It was now becoming late—I had been
there an hour; so I rose to say farewell to the lady,
and, after many compliments, we parted. It was a
far more amusing visit than most of those one pays
in London, where, in nine cases out of ten, it is impossible to say who is most *bored*, the visitor or the
visited.

I went through several rooms in this old palace; that in which the lady received me was very handsome and lofty, the ceilings richly carved and gilt, and round the cornices were Cufic inscriptions. The other rooms were similarly ornamented.

Our stay in Cairo was drawing to a close, yet there remained much that I was told I ought to see. We constantly heard — "Oh, you must not think of leaving Cairo without seeing this or that," and how often after leaving a place have 1 been asked if I had seen such and such an object? and on my perhaps answering -that I had not, have I been informed I had seen nothing !

The isle of Roda is very pretty, and the shade afforded by the numerous large trees there extremely pleasant on a hot day. These trees, however, like everything else in Egypt, are covered with dust, which penetrates into every corner of the dwelling-houses. There it can be in some measure remedied—not so in the mosques or streets, or on the trees, all of which are powdered over with sand, and everything looks dry, unrefreshed, and dirty.

It is in this island that tradition has placed the finding of Moses by Pharoah's daughter.

We did not fail to visit the Nilometer. Every morning during the inundation the daily rise of the Nile is announced in the streets of Cairo. The first Nilometer at Roda was built by Soolayman, who began his reign in A. D. 714.

There is also a modern palace in the island belonging to one of the many Egyptian pachas. We did not go in—for well I knew its contents: suites of large apartments, furnished in the worst possible modern French taste, with colours to set one's teeth on edge. So we preferred a walk in what remains of the pretty garden of Ibrahim Pacha.

There is, at Cairo, a girls'-school, in which Mrs. L., a lady long resident here, takes a very great interest. When we went there, we found many nice and good-looking little girls, seated on benches; among them Copts, Arabs, Syrians, Jewesses, Greeks, and Armenians. The teachers were Copt women. What a contrast in appearance were these children to those at the native school at Poona, I saw last year, with their short jackets, untidy hair, mouths and teeth stained red from chewing betle-nut and lime! These, on the contrary, had grace-ful and tidy dresses, long white veils, pearly teeth, and plaited tresses. One little Copt had on the 'safa.' It was composed of cords or strings of black silk, to which were attached small gold coins; and at the end of this 'safa' hung large pieces of money.

The Dervishes must not be forgotten. There is a college at Old Cairo, and a large convent at Grand Cairo for this class of devotees; neither of these did I visit, but we went on a Friday to a mosque at Old Cairo, to see the extraordinary manner in which these people perform their devotions. We were obliged to put on slippers, such being the rule whenever Franks go into any mosque here.

We found about forty men seated on furs in a circle. They were nearly all clad in dirty old garments, and some had on the dervish's high cap, much like a flower-pot reversed; others, the common turban worn here—a tarboosh surrounded by folds of cotton wound round it. The leader of the ceremonies, called the 'Sheikh,' stood in the middle of the circle. When we arrived, these poor fanatics were making the most extraordinary noises—all at the same moment sending forth a kind of low-toned, grumbling, groaning moan, as if they were in great bodily pain; but as they all altered this piteous cry at the same moment, it sounded like one monster growl. All the time they sat on the ground, they kept

swinging their bodies backwards and forwards.
This lasted about five minutes; then they rose,
and some took off their upper robes. Then the
sheikh began, in a more animated manner, to swing
his body, bowing his head lower and lower. The
others imitated his movements, still continuing
the same moan, which, by this time, I had discovered was 'Allah.'[1] Presently the sheikh's actions
became more violent; then a man began to play
on a reed or pipe; and the dervishes' bodies, like
that of their leader, bent quicker and quicker.
Then two men stepped out of the circle, and twirled
round like tops spinning, with their arms held
horizontally, with the palm of one hand down, and
the other up. Suddenly three strokes on a drum
were heard—bom, bom, bom; then a pause, then
three more strokes: the sheikh became excited,
and as the man piped on, and the drummer drum-
med on, the devotees looked wilder and wilder;
they threw their bodies and heads backwards and
forwards, nearly touching the ground with their

[1] This recalls to my mind what happened once when I
was in a boat on the canal between Cairo and Alexandria.
The boatmen, while rowing, are in the habit of singing in a
very low, mellow tone, 'Allah, Allah.' It is, though monotonous, soft, pleasing, musical, and soothing. A person said
to me—"Dear me! how like it is to 'Cherry Ripe'!"
(a popular song thirty years ago.)

foreheads one moment, and with the back of their
heads the next; their long, dishevelled hair tossed
to and fro, falling now over their faces, now down
their backs—they all looked like maniacs.   The
groans became quicker and deeper, the drums
louder, and the pipes shriller; and we were wondering what would come next, when one individual
fell back exhausted; the sheikh rushed forward,
and supported the fallen man's head, while the proceedings went on with, if possible, increased
vigour: when all was at the climax, in ran our
donkey-boys, and they, too joining the circle, began
moaning, and bowing, and bending; but *they* were
very awkward performers amongst these *artistes*,
whose bodies, from constant practice, have an elas-
ticity and suppleness perfectly astonishing.   As
these strange acts of devotion would continue
some time, and we knew there would be no variety
in them, we left, after being half an hour in the
mosque.

I was extremely amused; not so one of my companions, who wished to have left soon after the
proceedings began; but as I knew I should probably never return to Cairo, I thought it would be
a pity to lose the opportunity of seeing one of the
most curious sights of the place.

Before I left Cairo, I was fortunate enough to visit a Turkish lady, wife of a gentleman at that time high in favour with Abbas Pacha.

The house was large, and, as usual, built round a court-yard, in which two ostriches stalked about with a grave and measured tread, holding their heads high, and eyeing me in rather a suspicious manner; so that I was glad when a black male slave met me, and shewed the way through a very large hall to a broad staircase, which branched off at each side, leading up to a vestibule. Here, a frightful black woman came forward and conducted me into a drawing-room, which, but for its divans, I might have thought was in Europe, for there were chairs, a round table, and a book-case full of French works, whilst the walls covered with indifferent French prints—such as shepherdesses with big blue eyes, rosy lips and large hats. I was in despair, and thought to myself, where are Lane's 'leewans' (raised place to sit on), and the inlaid 'durkaah,' and the 'suffeh,' or shelf for the water-bottles? In this anything but Egyptian room I remained a few minutes, when the same ugly old black woman made me a sign to follow her. I did so, and it seemed as if I had been suddenly transported from a modern French inn to the abode of an Eastern lady.

The apartment was indeed an admirable specimen of an Egyptian dwelling, which had formerly belonged to one of the Memlook beys.

The lady of the house not being in the room, I had time to observe the decorations and style of furniture. The room itself was large, very lofty and well-proportioned. The ceiling of gopherwood, elaborately carved, and much gilt. Some of the colours on the ceiling had faded from age, but the beautiful blue was still fresh. Sentences from the Koran, in Cufic characters carved and gilt, were all round the cornices. To about four feet from the ground, the walls were of coloured marble in arabesque patterns. Above, there were coloured tiles, but these did not extend to any height. Near the entrance was a shelf of marble about four or five feet high, supported on arches; this is called the 'suffeh.' On it were some water-bottles. Opposite the door was a very large latticed window filling up one side of the room, and close under it the raised place to sit on, called 'leewan,' on it the divan. The part of the floor below the leewan was paved with coloured marbles, and also furnished with soft mattresses and cushions, covered with very handsome silk.

Shortly after my entrance the lady came into the room; the usual formal salutations followed. I touched her hand, raised my hand to my mouth, then to my forehead. She motioned me to sit on the divan, and on her left hand. The conversation flowed on for a short time pretty briskly through an interpreter, health and weather being the chief topics.

My hostess was exceedingly pretty, her complexion fair; she had small, delicate features, and an enchanting smile; and though very lively was dignified, the movement of her hands being most graceful. All her little sayings were prettily turned, and she looked so bright and intelligent, I could not help deploring her fate, and that she should remain half (if at all) educated, for reading a little and working was all she could do—she must live a regular Hareem life.

The war between England and Russia had not long commenced, this, therefore, was an interesting topic, and how the Turks (her husband was one) loved the English and French!

Her dress was very beautiful. The head-dress consisted, first, of a flat cap of horse-hair, through which her own hair peeped here and there; round this a green silk embroidered kerchief, tied on one side; on each side of her head were bouquets of very handsome diamonds. Her black hair was cut quite short over the forehead, but numerous long braids hung down behind. Her trowsers were wide and of white brocaded satin; the vest was of lilac silk, and fitted tight to her shape; round her waist was wound a small Cashmere shawl; the long 'gibbeh' of rich white embroidered satin covered her feet, on which were slippers; and a large, long, ample green Cashmere jacket, with full sleeves, completed this really becoming costume.

Presently, a sweet, rosy-cheeked little girl peeped in at the door; but when she caught a stranger's eye, away she ran. She was the lady's only daughter. The attendants pursued the timid little thing, and in vain endeavoured to coax her back.

It was now time for pipes and coffee, and sherbet. Black and white slaves entered—one carrying a large silver vessel, called 'azkee,' suspended by three chains, very pretty. This held the coffee-pot. Another slave held a silver tray with diminutive porcelain coffee-cups, placed in gilt filagree holders, called 'zarfs' (mine was adorned with diamonds); a third stood motionless with sherbet-cups on a tray, which was covered with a red velvet cloth embroidered in gold; a fourth approached with the pipes (mine, which I received from a sable damsel, was of purple enamel and gold, set with diamonds, the mouth-piece of amber). If a lady can be supposed to smoke with grace, my hostess certainly did so. She was much amused at the awkward manner in which I attempted to imitate her, and undertook to give me some instruction in this interesting art !—the lesson amusing her as much as it did me.

During this scene a young man about seventeen years of age, entered the room. The lady presented him to me as her son. He was a short, very stout, round, fat-faced youth, with small eyes, a smaller nose, and a still smaller mouth, and a little round chin, which he held constantly in the air. I could just trace a faint likeness to his lovely mother; but it was a sad caricature. He seated himself by me, and began a most energetic, animated conversation in French. I soon learned he had been long at Paris, where many young men of family now go from Egypt for their education.

His mother, on the other side of me, looked at him in silent admiration, though she did not understand one word he said; and it was very strange to sit between the mother and son. The first realizing all one has heard of Eastern customs and manners, which are the same as those of three hundred years ago, while the son, aware his country was behind European nations in *all respects*, was panting for emancipation from these very customs. He told me he was extremely '*bored*' in Cairo. "Il n'y a pas de société ici, madame; point de *whisk* (whist)." He then rattled on about his happy life in Paris. In vain I tried to smooth matters, and make him see the '*bright side*' of Cairo. He evidently looked down on his country, and wanted reforms. Here I had before me a specimen of '"young Egypt,' and I thought what a pity it was to send youths out of the country to be half-civilized, when they must return and conform, during the rest of their lives, to the demi-barbarous customs of their own land, The poor young man's love of his country did not increase, when he was suddenly informed he must at once leave the apartment.

"Madame," said he, "il faut que je quitte la chambre—chez nous les messieurs et les dames n'osent pas rester dans la même chambre. Il y a une dame qui arrive et qui desire entrer ici pour voir ma mère—et moi, je suis forcé de quitter la chambre. Ah! nous tenons cette coutume des anciens Grecs."

I did not know how the custom originated,

but I thought it rather hard to put it on the Greeks.

As soon as he had left, the Egyptian, or rather Turkish, lady came in. She was an ancient lady, tall, stately, and most particularly ugly. I thought the young man might have remained after all, as the visitor was by no means dangerous.

She was dressed like all Egyptian ladies when they go out. A pair of yellow leather boots met the wide silk trowsers, and over all she wore a large loose fawn-coloured silk robe with sleeves, (nearly equal to the whole length of the gown), which is called a 'tob;' a kerchief was tied round the tarboosh, a head-veil hung down behind, while another kerchief tied up her cheeks and chin, and was fastened on the top of the head. She seemed to take no interest in anything, and to care very little for the outer world—a great contrast to 'young Egypt.'

The lady of the house offered to show me her other rooms, and led me by one hand, the other being occupied in keeping the 'gibbeh' up, lest she should tread on it. It can be well imagined that such a costume does not contribute to a graceful gait.

The bath-room had a beautiful ceiling of carved stone. The bath was of marble. The other rooms, though simple, were handsome, and furnished with divans. The bed-room almost European.

The little frightened daughter at last ventured to approach us. She was worth seeing; her dress was like that of her mother, as to make; as to material, all was of lilac Cashmere, richly embroidered in gold, and the little thing dressed out in its 'best,' had even a train like its mother. On her head was a tarboosh of red velvet, embroidered in gold, and a chain of pearls with a diamond ornament suspended from it; but, at the end of the rich brocaded trowsers, what was there? Scotch plaid warm socks, and a pair of European buttoned boots!

She was plump—very plump—and bid fair to be like her brother, 'young Egypt,' eventually, though she was a lovely child. She was attended by several black and white slaves, who pursued her from corner to corner; and she could not escape from their surveillance; the 'gibbeh' would have tripped her up, had she made a hasty retreat.

After I took leave of the lady, the young man met me—offering me his arm to take me to my donkey—(*not* to my carriage). Having been banished from the hareem, he was not in a better humour with his country, and lamented bitterly the *triste* life he led, and the dullness of Cairo. I was sorry for him; and have often thought since what has become of him?

Having seen much on this side of the Nile, we thought it was time to cross the river and visit the Pyramids of Geezeh. Our intentions, however, were nearly being frustrated—for the little steamer in which we embarked at Boulac narrowly escaped being annihilated by a large one coming down the river from Upper Egypt. This was rather too exciting and stirring an event to be pleasant. The strange vessel, fortunately, checked its speed in time; and, in passing each other, some very *civil* words were exchanged between the captains; but, from what I could understand of the case (which was very little, however) our commander was not to blame. After these gentlemen had exhausted their angry invectives, we went on our way. We scarcely lost sight of the citadel, or the dome of the new mosque and its minarets, till we reached the Pyramids, so that, looking back, we had a pleasing picture nearly all the way.

At the village of Geezeh we left the steamer, and found our donkeys ready. We were a large party, and the ride was most agreeable.

Geezeh is as ruinous as villages in Egypt generally are. One could scarcely think that a city
with the palaces of the Memlooks had once stood
here! After wandering among Geezeh's crumbling
walls, and wretched hovels, we came on the open
plain—passed by well-cultivated fields—and, what
with the singing birds, the sweet flowers, and the
fresh, spring-like air (perhaps a little too brisk for
us lately come from India), I felt I could have
ridden on to the centre of Africa without stopping.

The dwellings of the Egyptian peasantry are mere
mud hovels; there is a hole for a door, but no
windows. Dogs abound everywhere, and they rush
out barking at all who pass by. Children, with
flies nearly concealing their features, lie like pigs
deeply set in mire; men stand smoking at their
doors, while the women are to be seen with water
vessels on their heads, often one child on the
shoulder, and leading another by the hand. The
women do not wear the face-veil so much as they do
in the city; they have the yackmac, which they
wrap close round their faces when a stranger approaches. We met no horses; camels and donkeys
generally carry everybody and everything in Egypt;
priests, sultanas, and sellers of chairs, all ride
donkeys.

Every now and then we caught a view of the
three Pyramids as we rode over the plain, passing by
groves of date-palms, which are not nearly so
picturesque as those trees are in India. The fertile
fields extend as far as the low sandy hills on which
are the Pyramids and Sphinx; at last we found
ourselves close to the large Pyramid, and were soon
surrounded by numerous Arabs, some speaking a word
or two of English, all proffering their services, and
becoming every minute more troublesome. The
view looking towards Cairo from the stony, sandy
ground close to the great Pyramid is very beautiful. A wide extent of plain runs up to the Nile;
the villages, dotted about among groves of palms,
looked to advantage at a distance, for we did not
see the ruined houses, walls, and heaps of rubbish
of which they were composed. Cairo, backed by the
Mokuttum range of hills, looked well—even grand—
for you did not perceive that many of the mosques are
in ruins, nor the crumbling walls, dilapidated houses,
dusty-coloured trees, and sandy ground around the
city. It looked like a city of mosques, minarets,
and palaces; and between the plain and city
flowed the river, sometimes hidden by gardens and
groves of trees. The citadel and large mosque
were in a brilliant light; and the day was fine, with

a soft blue sky shading into the horizon with a faint and indescribable tint, something between a very pale plumbago and the softest possible French grey.

Many are the strange and interesting reflections which come across one in contemplating these wonderful buildings the Pyramids, concerning which so much has been written, while there are still so many different opinions as to the purpose for which they were erected.

But it was now time to enter the great Pyramid. The Arab guides came round us like a swarm of flies. I little thought what would follow, and at first refused all assistance from these people, who seemed to stand aghast when I began scrambling alone over high stones to get to the entrance of the Pyramid, which is more like a hole than a door: round it the Arabs were crowding like ants at their nests—all talking at the same time in a loud voice, each trying to talk down his neighbour. Groping through the door, and following men with lighted candles, I found a slippery descent, at once fell flat on my face, and was picked up by two strong Arabs, whose help I had despised at first, but whom I was grateful to find near me. I was supported on each side by these men, while another remained close by to assist me if I fell.

All this time my companions were close behind me, aided, or carried on, like myself. The dust raised by so many feet, and the excessive heat of the confined passages, was very overpowering; besides, the noise and loud wild voices of the guides were quite deafening, and the murky darkness, relieved only by the flickering light of the numerous candles, most bewildering. Still, we went on till we came to a level spot, where we rested. I was breathless; our labours were but begun—and what had we seen? Nothing. I had to climb up about four feet, which I accomplished by the help of the Arabs—then to ascend a steeply-inclined, polished slab, or rather shelf. While doing this, an enthusiastic individual cried out to me to look somewhere, for there was the entrance to the passage leading to what is called the 'Queen's Chamber;' but my energy and enthusiasm were nearly worn out, and, I fear, the horrible wish entered my head, that Cheops had never built this Pyramid! Still, on I went, supported by Arabs; one saying, to encourage me—" Good lady ! good lady !" the other crying out—" Good Arab, give good Arab backshish."

At last, after more climbing, slipping, and stooping, we reached the 'King's Chamber.' As each of us arrived in turn, all the Arabs raised a shout of triumph, and I was so overjoyed, I made a feeble attempt to join them. Our party nearly filled the chamber. My guides amused me extremely, though they gave me not a moment's peace asking for 'backshish.' One at last, patting me on the back, whispered—"Lady, more backshish."

The chamber is about thirty-four feet long, seventeen broad, and nineteen high. The roof is flat. The sarcophagus, which is much damaged, is about seventeen feet long, and three wide, and is at the upper end of the chamber. After resting a short time, we recommenced our labours, which were pretty much of the same character as when we entered the Pyramid; again was I rash enough to try and go alone, and, consequently, at the spot where I before fell on my face, I now fell on my back.

How glad I was to see daylight!

Had any one asked me, when I came out, what 1 had seen—I should have said, "Only an old stone trough!"

After such exertion I need scarcely say that refreshments were by no means unacceptable. While the energetic members of our party climbed up to the summit of the Pyramid, I took a sketch of Cairo in the distance. Of course, when our friends came down, I was told, "I had seen nothing," as I had not followed their example and climbed to the summit; but this did not signify, I had seen the 'old stone trough,' and that was quite enough for me.

We walked round the base of the great Pyramid and looked at the other two, then went to the Sphinx, which I had been more anxious to see (if possible) than the Pyramids.

After staring and wondering for some time at the enormous head and shoulders of this colossal figure, I could not help asking where was "the bland repose and immutable serenity of countenance," of which I had heard so much? The face is much mutilated, and devoid of any vestige of nose, and the lips, though 1 may be contradicted by many, are decidedly and coarsely African. I made a sketch both of its full face and profile; and a nearer acquaintance did not induce me to agree with those who are enraptured with its fine expression and " God-like benignity." [1] We returned to

_____

[1] An old admiral, who came from his ship at Alexandria to see the Pyramids, was asked, when he got back to Malta, what he had seen? "Nothing," he replied, "but a con-

the steamer in the evening, and as I had ridden and walked several miles, I was very tired.

We remained on board during the night, as we were to go to the Pyramids of Sakkara and Memphis the following day. Accordingly, at five A.M., we proceeded in the steamer to the spot were we could most conveniently land, in order to reach Sakkara.

We had a letter of introduction to a French gentleman, who was employed by his government, with the permission, of course, of the Pacha of Egypt, to make some excavations; and we had heard so much of their interesting nature that we were most desirous of seeing them. Besides, the idea of passing the site of Memphis, the Nopf of Scripture, with all its history fresh in one's mind, was almost enough to keep one awake all night; so I was glad when we reached the shore, mounted our donkeys, and went on our way to Mitrahenny, which is universally believed to be the centre of Memphis.

This city is said to have been built by Menes, who reigned 2320 B.C., thus being even older than the great Pyramid we saw yesterday, the date assigned to which is 2123 B.C.

Memphis had many names. Among the ancient founded great stone they call a Spix." He evidently had seen nothing of its " calm sublimity."

Egyptian ones, some, when translated, are very pretty. One is, " The place of Good ;" then it was called, " The Land of the Pyramid ;" " The City of the White Wall."

In Isaiah xix. 13, it is Nopf; and in Hosea ix. 6, Memphis ; when the prophet, in uttering the judgment of God on Ephraim, says, " For lo, they are gone because of destruction, Egypt shall gather them up, Memphis shall bury them." It was the capital of Lower Egypt, and here Apis received most special worship and honour.

The desolation of Egypt by Nebuchadnezzar, and that " Noph shall have distresses daily," were prophesied in Ezekiel xxx. 16 ; but it was Cambyses who ravaged and nearly destroyed Memphis and its temples. As late, however, as 1342, the city was extensive, though its grandeur and glory had departed. Nothing now remains to give one any idea of its beauty and magnificence.

Dusty mounds and wretched hovels of Egyptian peasants, bits of granite, groves of date trees, remains of one or two figures, now cover the site of palaces, temples, and statues. There is one solitary colossal statue, believed to be that of Remeses the second, better known as the great Sesostris, the conqueror of Syria and India. It is in a pit, which, even at that dry season, was nearly full of water, so that during the inundations poor Remeses must be in a perpetual bath. Its height is somewhere about forty-two feet, and the face, which is in remarkably good preservation, is evidently the portrait of a man with fine dignified features.

The statue was given to the English nation many years ago by old Mahomet Ali, and if we do not think proper to remove it, we ought, at least, I think, to take measures to avert the risk which is now imminent of its being defaced or seriously damaged.

For many years its identity was doubted. It had been called Sesostris on the authority of a passage in Strabo, who describes a statue of that monarch standing near a temple, his account of the situation of which tallies exactly with the mounds about Mitrahenny. Strabo also describes colossal statues of the monarch's wife and his children, as standing near Sesostris' own statue. It was not till the year in which we were there, that it occurred to an Armenian gentleman (named Hakeekyan Bey,) that if the great statue were that of Sesostris, some remains of the other statues of his family might be found in the positions assigned to them by Strabo. He got permission to dig, and was rewarded by finding the greater portion of each of the three statues, prostrate, indeed, and much defaced, but in sufficiently good preservation to leave no doubt of their being the statues he sought, and to enable him to complete the gallery of family portraits.

After paying our respects to the fallen monarch, we hurried on, not to enter a pyramid—for I had had enough of that—but to the curious and deeply interesting excavations going on at Sakkara.

The French gentleman, M. Marietti, who was employed there, had built for himself a small house of the ancient Egyptian bricks; he received us in his little neat and retired home—and retired indeed it was—his *nearest neighbours* being sacred bulls, mummies; and tombs and graves touching the very threshold of his door. It might well be said of him, " his dwelling was among the tombs." He was good enough to have the excavations lighted up for us.

They consist of long galleries cut out of the limestone rock. The entrances are sunk below the surface of the ground, which is here covered to the depth of many feet by the moving sands of the desert, and their discovery, after being concealed for so many centuries, was a great triumph of the antiquarian sagacity of Monsieur Marietti.

Strabo had described them as they had existed in his day. He gave their distance and bearing from certain points in Memphis, and told how even then the advancing sand-hills of the Libyan Desert threatened to entomb the avenue of sphinxes which led up to the entrance. Monsieur Marietti, after carefully examining the ground, selected a spot, where he began to dig, apparently in the fathomless sand, and, of course, incurred much ridicule from his antiquarian friends; but he was soon rewarded by finding first one sphinx, and then another, and at last the whole avenue. They are not monstrous colossi, like the sphinxes near the Pyramid of Cheops, but comparatively small, tame specimens of their race; and had we not been specially introduced to them, they might have passed for fresh arrivals from the tops of the gate-posts of some suburban villa near London. However, they led Monsieur M. to the entrance of the sepulchres of Apis. These consist of long galleries, about twenty feet high, and the same in width. On either side is a row of large chambers, sunk to a depth of several feet below the floor of the gallery; and each chamber contains a single sarcophagus, in which once reposed the mummy of a sacred · bull. The sarcophagi are generally of black granite (though there are a few of grey and red granite), of vast dimensions; twelve feet long, by eight high, and eight wide, with sides, and a lid eighteen inches thick, is a common size: and we saw remains of a temporary table, on which the hospitable antiquary had given a dinner to five of his friends, *inside* one of the sarcophagi, to celebrate, I believe, the deportation of the original tenant to the Museum of the Louvre. Perhaps the poor animal was lucky in not being called on to furnish any portion of the feast, like the antediluvian ox, whose bones were discovered by a learned geologist in a cave in Yorkshire, and which he delighted in proving to his friends still contained much of their original gelatine. There are two or three exceptions to the size of the sarcophagi. These probably belonged to some calf Apis, who died after his election, but before arriving at his full growth.

The sarcophagi are generally plain, but a few are inscribed with very minute and delicately cut hieroglyphics. Their great bulk, and the difficulty of getting them out of their present confined position, has hitherto prevented their removal.

When he first reached these sepulchral galleries, Monsieur Marietti was much disappointed to find that he was not the first profane intruder who had come there to disturb the resting place of the sacred bulls. All the tombs which were visible on a first inspection had been opened, the lids of the sarcophagi raised or moved aside, and the bull mummies which were probably very richly ornamented, had been removed. It is conjectured that this occurred during the visit of Cambyses. At length, by dint of very careful search, the French antiquary discovered two cells untouched, which he opened, and found to contain the bull mummies in exactly the same state as when they were buried, and it is supposed that he obtained from them a number of articles of great antiquarian interest. But on this subject he maintained a discreet silence. The export of antiquities from Egypt is nominally prohibited, and though everything portable of real interest disappeared almost as soon as it was discovered, and a French vessel of war carried away from Alexandria numerous mysterious cases, it was not till they arrived at the Louvre that the full value of Monsieur M.'s excavations became known even to his brother antiquaries in Egypt.

When thinking of that marvellous place, and that no doubt can be entertained but that a conqueror ravaged those tombs, how instantly the prophecy concerning Memphis naturally recurs to the memory. "I will destroy the idols, and I will cause their images to cease out of Nopf." [1]

There are many pyramids to be seen and visited in the neighbourhood of Geezeh and Sakkara. There are big pyramids, middle-sized pyramids, and little pyramids, some of stone and some of brick; but I had read so much about them, of their dimensions, and for what use they were supposed to have been erected, and for what use they were not, that I was rather tired of pyramids; and we determined to ride back to the steamer and return to Cairo.

[1] Ezekiel xxx. 13.

CHAPTER VI.

IT was on a very cold day, in the month of February, that we left Cairo for Thebes.

We were fortunate in having a steamer, which the Pacha had most kindly lent us. In addition to our own servants, we took the Janissary who had attended on us during our stay in Cairo, a French washerwoman, and her son, who promised to assist everybody, but who, instead of fulfilling his engagement, was in every one's way, did nothing, and was a very naughty boy.

We passed quickly the pretty island of Roda,

old Cairo, Geezeh, and were soon in Upper Egypt, known as " Saeed."

The voyage up the Nile is almost as easily accomplished now, as that up the Rhine to Mayence. So many go every year to Thebes, and so few return from thence without giving to the world a volume of either "Notes," "Fragments," or "Sketches," written on the Nile, that the narrative of an excursion thither can scarcely be made to present any features of novelty.

The legend of Gebel e' Tayr (mountain of the bird) is as familiar to us all as the romantic tales of Liebenstein, Drachenfels, and Rolandsack.

The hall of Karnak, and all the temples, with the Osirtasens, Thothmeses, and Ptolemies, are as well known as those lovely ruins on the Rhine, with the tales of their heroines, Knights of the Temple, counts, and barons.

Everybody has heard of the Dom palm, and of its graceless stiff boughs, and fan-shaped leaves— of the lofty pigeon-houses, which, at a distance, I took for " pylons" and " pyramidal towers," of the muddy banks of the Nile, with the lazy crocodiles lying on them ; and of the ancient names of all the different places where travellers stop during the voyage. I shall therefore relate my impressions of our tour to Upper Egypt as briefly as possible.

It was late in the year for a large steamer to ascend the Nile, and we therefore hastened on to Asouan, only stopping *en route* to take in coal at three or four places, intending to visit on our return all the wonders we left behind us.

The first place at which we stopped to coal was Esné, when the Janissary came to me and said, "Timbels here." "What are timbles?" I inquired. "*Antikities are timbels*," was his reply. So we went on shore, and walked ancle deep in dust to visit the temple of Esné, or rather its portico, for what is supposed still to exist of the body of the temple is buried under mounds of rubbish, or concealed by the hovels of the peasantry.

This was our introduction to Egyptian ' Antikity.' I forgot at first I was in Egypt, and thought Siva, Vishnoo, or the elephant-headed god, would greet me when I entered the portico; but none of 'the old familiar faces' were there. Instead of Gunputty, there was a stranger with a ram's head, who, I learnt, is called Knepf, and who, although met with in other temples, was the presiding deity of ancient Esné.

Every part of this portico, inside and out, is covered with hieroglyphics.

There are many beautiful columns, the capitals of

which are not all alike; but the lotus and palm leaves are among their principal ornaments, the colours in parts being still visible.

Nothing of any moment occurred between Esné and Asouan, save meeting boats returning from, or overtaking others going up to, the cataracts.

As we approached Asouan, the scenery became gradually more pleasing. It is indeed only at that place on the Nile that it is so; but as we anchored close to the shore, the views up and down the river were really picturesque.

There were sandy hills in the distance, with rather a cold blue sky behind; but near there were high banks with ruined buildings on them, small rocky islands dotted about, and the island of Elephantine opposite the town.

Having procured horses and donkeys, we rode to Philæ. The donkey-boy, who ran by my side, had two leather bags tied round his throat. I found, on enquiry, that his spiritual adviser had placed in them bits of paper, with words written on them, which he said were charms against the poor boy's falling ill.

The road to Philæ was desolate—covered with old tombs in ruins, and heaps of rocks; whilst very few trees or plants were to be seen.

We entered a boat, and soon saw a small island covered with rocks, piled one upon another, out of which rose a few solitary palms; and at last we caught sight of a temple, the pillars appearing sunk in the wild confusion around them, and buried among masses of granite. The island was the far-famed Philæ, and the temple that of Isis.

The banks of the river are all of the same character—barren, cold, and wild, without being grand.

The scenery has, in my opinion, been over-rated. I do not think it deserves to be called ' beautiful.'

There is one lovely 'bit,' where the building, known by the name of ' Pharoah's Bed,' is placed. It stands overlooking the water, and surrounded by trees, which cover also the high bank down to the edge of the river. We remained at Philæ several hours, wandering among its ruins, and through the large temple commenced by Ptolemy Philadelphus and Arsinoëe, examining the sculptures on the walls, where the death and resurrection of Osiris are por-trayed ; then those relating to the birth of Horus, the son of Osiris and Isis ; admiring the still vivid blue colouring of the ornaments of the capitals of the columns ; visiting the small chapel of Esculapius, and another dedicated to Athor.

The walls of Pharoah's Bed were disfigured with the names of travellers. This bad taste was formerly confined to the English. Other nations have followed our example, and in almost all the Egyptian ruins one may see the most romantic and aristocratic name by the side of that of Thomas Biggs, from Philadelphia, United States, and perchance that of Prince Puckler Muskau close to that of William Button, from Cheapside, London.

Towards the evening, we left this fabled burial-place of Osiris, and determined to return to Asouan by water, descending the cataract.

Having taken in a pilot, the boat being carefully trimmed, and 'womankind' desired to sit still, and ' *not make a fuss,*' we moved off from the shore.

We had about twenty-five boatmen: they began to row with vigour—all talking, and seeming to give orders—apparently everything was confusion. As we advanced, the men became more noisy; and not only talked, but shouted, and screamed: the pilot stood up shouting and screaming louder than anyone. All around us were gushing, foaming, and seemingly contending currents tearing over and under the rocks, against masses of which it appeared as if we must inevitably be dashed; still the boat proceeded smoothly, though with extreme and almost frightful rapidity, and somehow or other we escaped a collision of any kind, till we reached the brink of the fall, or rapid, when the stern rose high, and for a moment, the bows of the vessel appeared to plunge into the watery abyss; suddenly, the prow emerged almost perpendicularly from the water, of which a good deal had entered the boat, and after two or three more or less violent plunges and struggles were over, the gunwale became level, and we could stand upright without support; the cataract was passed, but the shouting ceased not, and though the pilot called out all was right, and that all danger (if there had been any), had ceased, my excitement continued, for the speed with which we had descended, still impelled the boat, and it seemed as if the boatmen had lost all command over it; this, however, was not the case, and the way in which they guided it, and avoided the labyrinth of rocks was marvellous. These soon became fewer, the water calmer, the shouting and howling less, the men brought the boat close to a bank, and all was over. I felt sorry that it was so.

We visited Elephantine, where are some ruins and a gigantic statue of granite, which I had time to sketch, and which, though not very beautiful, was far more so than the Nubian ladies of the island, whom travellers have called '*elegant in their appearance*,' though some one has said, '*that their beauty is over-rated.*' Their features are very African, the women small and thin, they wear very little covering, but a great number of necklaces and coloured beads and shells, their limbs are well oiled, and their hair smeared with ointment, which renders them more agreeable when at a distance, than when near.

Leaving Asouan, we now bent our course down the river, visiting on our way to Thebes, such temples and grottoes as were worth seeing.

When we wished to land, the captain naturally thought of his ship, and where we could best anchor, he therefore did not always stop near the village from whence the Janissary had to procure donkeys to take us to the different places, and our friend, Abousaid, not liking such long walks, often tried to persuade us from going on shore, saying, " you go four mile, and then see only mud-wall, *she* not worth seeing."

One evening, when we had, perhaps, anchored unnecessarily far from the place where the donkeys were to be obtained, and Abousaid had gone in search of them, we landed, and walked to meet them. We soon heard, though we did not see the Janissary, for his loud voice betokened he was in a

great state of excitement, and was evidently pour-
ing his grievances into the donkey-boys' ears.
Settled on our donkeys, Abousaid on before us,
and I heard him say to himself—"Captain very
foolish; he makes himself know everything." I
remarked that when he could lay nothing to the
captain's charge, he used to say—"Captain is
Albanian. All Albanian bad."

We little heeded Abousaid's evident dislike to
'mud walls, timbels, and antikities,' and proceeded
to visit them all, beginning with the temple of
Kom Ombo, which is situated near the river. In
this temple we made acquaintance with Savak, the
deity with a crocodile's head, and the hawk-
headed god[1] of the Egyptians. Although this
building is of the time of Ptolemy Philometer, it
is satisfactory to antiquaries that there is a stone
gateway of the time of Thothmes the Third.

We did not forget the grottoes and chapels of
Hagar Silsileh, where the sculptured walls were
curious, and the subjects new to us.

In one grotto, commenced by Horus, who reigned
1408 B.C., is represented that monarch's victory
over the Ethiopians; and in a chapel of Remeses
the king presents offerings to all the numerous

[1] Symbolical of the sun.

deities—among them 'the Lord of Ombos,' the crocodile-headed god.

The large temple of Edfoo is magnificent. It is very extensive, and gives one a complete idea of what these wonderful edifices must have been when perfect. The brilliant turquoise blue of the ceilings in the corridors is as fresh in parts as when the artist first painted them in the time of Ptolemy Philometer, who founded this temple.

The walls in the corridors are covered with scenes representing the king returning victorious from battle.

Although there had been hitherto so much to call forth our admiration, nothing engaged my attention so much as the paintings in the tombs of El Kab. The first sculptured grotto contains the names of monarchs who reigned from 1575 B.C. to 1456 B.C.

The subjects of the paintings in one large tomb are highly interesting, from the insight they give into the common habits of life of the Egyptians, at so early a period as the eighteenth dynasty, permitting us to see exactly how they ploughed and reaped, fowled and fished, between fourteen and fifteen hundred years before our Saviour; and to know how their boats, threshing floors, and wine-presses, were constructed.

Not less curious are the scenes of in-door life

on the opposite wall, on which the host and hostess are depicted receiving their guests. The festive board is spread; there is a band of musicians; and among the instruments played on is the harp. Neither is it uninteresting to know that there were 'pets' in the time of Moses, for we perceive a little monkey, chained to a lady's arm-chair, in which she is sitting. And there was the procession of the bier when the owner of the tomb is carried off to his 'long home.'

Erment, built by the celebrated Cleopatra, must have been a beautiful temple.

The bull was particularly adored here, and the queen is seen on the walls worshipping that animal. Tradition says that Moses was born at Erment.

The time was not long enough to admit of my satisfying my curiosity, and when I returned to the steamer, I thought I had seen very little, although I groped into every grotto, crept into every sanctuary, squeezed into every hole, and pryed into every chamber.

We had now several days reserved for Thebes.

All the world is aware that Thebes is the No of scripture,[1] and that it was prophesied that the Lord God would cut off the multitude of No.

[1] Jeremiah xlvi.—25.
In the third chapter of Nahum, where the miserable ruin

Luxor and Karnak are near the river, and as this enabled us to go often to them, I passed several evenings among their beautiful colonades and extensive courts. But the grand hall at Karnak should be seen the last. No description, no drawing, can give any idea of its magnificence and vastness. It contains one hundred and thirty-four columns, twelve of which are sixty-six feet high, and twelve in diameter, the others are rather smaller.

They do not all stand erect; but though some are fallen, and some prevented from doing so by those still upright, enough remain perpendicular to prevent the effect being spoilt, and to give one an idea of what this hall—built by Osirei, 1380 B.C.— must have been, with the enormous gateway, area, avenue of sphinxes and colossi, some of which, however, were added by succeeding monarchs.

The other buildings are of a much earlier period; and there are a few columns of the date of Osis-tasen—the Pharoah of Joseph's time.

There are the usual subjects sculptured on the

of Nineveh is foretold, we read, " Art thou better than populous No, that was situated among the rivers, that had the rivers round about it, whose rampart was the sea, and her wall was from the sea?" "Ethiopia and Egypt were her strength, and it was infinite."

walls of the temples; some of the sculptures in the great hall having relation to Osirei the First's campaigns in the East.

On one wall we see the Egyptians victorious; the enemy routed. Sir Gardner Wilkinson observes— "The name of the town (Kanana), and the early date of the first year of the king's reign, leave little room to doubt that the defeat of the Canaanites is here represented."

One more sculpture in this hall, where the Egyptians are seen following the enemy into woods, particularly attracted my attention. "The trees," as Sir Gardner Wilkinson remarks, "here represented, are probably cedars, the place being evidently called Lebanon, or, as the hieroglyphics write it, 'Lemanon.'"

Besides the buildings at Luxor and Karnak, there were graceful obelisks to be admired; gigantic, sitting statues, and couchant sphinxes to be wondered at—although some were headless and others with mutilated limbs.

In the middle of the plain, on the side of the river, opposite to where Karnak and Luxor stand, are THE Colossi—one of which was the well-known vocal Memnon.

Although they were not very near any temples,

many are visible from thence; among them Medee-net Haboo, the Memnonium, and, in the distance, Karnak and Luxor.

During my stay at Thebes, I often visited these statues. I was with them at sunrise, returned to them at sunset, and was never weary of looking at them in the evening; they seemed to have increased in size since the morning, and to look even grander; for as the sun declined, they were magnificent as they sat, two dark-purple masses against the radiant golden sky, with their shadows sweeping across the plain, and seemingly lost in the river. There have they sat on their thrones, or chairs, since Amunoph (who began to reign not many years after the death of Moses) placed them there, and they look deter-mined to sit the world out! They are much muti-lated, and there is scarcely a traceable feature. "The height of either Colossus is forty-seven feet, or fifty-three above the plain, with the pedestal, which, now buried from six feet ten inches to seven feet below the surface, completes its base—a total of sixty feet."[1] The body of the vocal statue has been repaired with blocks of sandstone.

I sketched these figures from all sides of the plain; their backs, at a distance, had a very droll

[1] Sir Gardner Wilkinson.

effect—they looked like old men sitting in arm-chairs, and wearing wigs and pigtails.

We spent one day in examining the temple-palace, begun by Osirei at Old Koorneh; passed another day in admiring the Memnonium and its beautiful sculptures, and deplored the fate of the statue of (I think) Remeses the Second. That mighty monarch lies on his back, deprived of his legs, and his majesty's head has furnished mill-stones for the peasantry of the surrounding villages.

We paid a lengthened visit to the temple-palace of Remeses the Third, at Medeenet Haboo. Here were sculptures, representing domestic scenes. The king is in the hareem; he sits while the ladies stand; some of them give him flowers, others fan him, and a game of draughts is represented.

We had become acquainted with the principal temples at Thebes, had seen Osirei, and other Egyptian monarchs in their private life, their peaceful royal state, or returning in all their pomp and glory as victors from distant lands, we now followed them to where they " slept with their fathers," and entered the Tombs of the Kings.

There required lights before we entered the chambers where so many of the Pharoahs were buried.

We were struck with the bright colours on the pillars, walls, and especially on the ceilings, some of which were of a rich blue, spangled over with gold stars.

In the tomb known by the name of Belzoni's tomb, (he having excavated it) we no longer see Osirei as a great conqueror, but are introduced into the presence of Osiris and Isis by their son Horus.

In the Harpers' Tomb (so called from two figures on the walls playing harps) there was a great deal to arrest our attention. On the walls were shewn in detail the operations of the kitchen and bakery, and we saw also the sort of chairs and couches the ancient Egyptians sat on, the coats of mail they wore, the vases of porcelain, the baskets they carried, with many other objects of domestic use.

We visited many tombs, but time did not admit of our going into every one of the numerous sepulchres of the many Remeses, we felt it a duty however to go to those of the Queens, but we found there nothing particularly interesting. We had lived among the royal tombs so long, that I was beginning to be rather tired of them, and was glad to visit those of the priests, and other private

individuals at the Assaseef and the hill of El Koorneh, of which the latter are especially worthy of notice.

The frescoes represent a variety of subjects and
objects we had not seen elsewhere.   There are
persons busy in various trades.   On one wall a
variety of female ornaments, on another, the
customs followed at their festivities are painted
in minute detail.   And in one chamber there
are foreigners presenting tributes to the Egyptian
monarch, Thothmes the Third.

These foreigners are evidently of distinct nations.
Their dress and complexions being different.
Among the offerings are ebony, ivory, ostrich-eggs,
hounds, oxen, and apes.

On our way back to Cairo we did not omit to go
to Dendera and the grottos of Beni Hassan.

The temple at the former is the only one we saw
with a roof.   The portico is extremely fine ; its
numerous columns, however, are far from graceful,
and they are not improved by their capitals bearing
heads of Athor with heavy drapery.

The oldest name here is that of Ptolemy Neo-
Cæsar, son of the famous Cleopatra, whose portrait
is on the wall outside of the temple.

Mounds of earth are frequently heaped up as
high as the roof of these buildings.   This helped

me to enter an aperture in the wall nearly at the top of the temple; when inside, I found myself in narrow, gently descending passages (the walls of which were covered with hieroglyphics); they led down into the body of the temple.

While rambling in the dark chambers, which are rendered more mysterious here than in any other temple, for all is covered in, I saw a square opening in the wall which can scarcely be called anything more than a hole. I felt I should have been wanting in spirit and energy had I not gone in, so sending in a guide before me with a light, I thought of how I should enter this singular place. Having contrived to get in, I began, when about half way through, to repent of my rashness; but there was no room to turn. So on I went; how I got through I cannot well remember, but it must have been on my knees and the palms of my hands. And I had no sooner got on my feet, than a large bat hit my head, and nearly put out the light held by the guide.

I then discovered a long, seemingly never-ending passage, inhabited by a world of bats, which flew up and down, apparently amazed at being disturbed.

On the walls of this passage were hieroglyphics

deeply engraven; and, from its secluded position, they were quite perfect.

The crocodile in ancient Dendera (the name of which was Tentyris) was as much an object of horror as it was of reverence at Kom Ombos.

It is said that the inhabitants of Tentyris, having once killed a crocodile, a fearful war raged in consequence between them and the Ombites. Which party was victorious I do not know.

At the grottoes of Beni Hassan, lower down the Nile, we found a curious scene portrayed on the walls—a number of men and women being beaten, the former receiving their punishment with their faces on the ground, the latter treated with more deference; they sit while their chastisement is given on the shoulders.

But it is time to finish my Nile-boat adventures, and this uninteresting account of an excursion, which has been made and described so often, that little now remains to be told. The Chow-Chow basket, however, would have been incomplete without it, and I have felt obliged, therefore, to leave a corner for this heavy chapter.

CHAPTER VII.

WE remained a long and tedious fortnight at Alexandria, waiting for a steamer to take us to Joppa, now, often called Jaffa.

Alexandria has few attractions. The town struck us as particularly uninteresting, after having passed so much time at Cairo; and, recollecting its early history, and ancient prosperity and magnificence, we could not help contrasting them with its present condition, so different from what it was when taken by Amer, who wrote to his sovereign

Omar, "I have taken the great city of the west, which contains 4000 palaces, 4000 baths, 400 theatres, 12,000 shops for vegetable food, and 40,000 tributary Jews."

Of the ancient town there are scarcely any vestiges remaining. Pompey's Pillar and the obelisk, called Cleopatra's Needle, look *almost* as much out of place in this Europeanized town as they would in High Holborn!

There are no mosques worth visiting—not a picturesque building to admire. You find the dust and dirt of Cairo without that city's picturesque streets and houses. In the Frank quarter are a few rather good houses, and a. Protestant church, which will be handsome when finished; but the Roman Catholic and Greek churches are unsightly.

There is a large house belonging to the pacha, decorated and furnished in the same manner as all the enormous palaces at Cairo.

Alexandria was unusually animated when we were there; the son of the Pacha had been bethrothed to a daughter of the reigning Sultan, and preparations were going on for an illumination.

I asked Abousaid if he meant to join in the general rejoicing.

" No, lady—what care I for Abbas Pacha's son?

when *Roosians* all dead, then I light up my house."

The Protestant, Syrian, Roman Catholic, and Greek cemeteries are at some little distance from the town, and only separated from each other by walls.

One day I saw a singular funeral procession leaving the town. A monk on a donkey was leading; behind, followed a Janissary, riding on a similar animal; then some little boys on foot, wearing white muslin scarfs, and bouquets of green leaves fastened in front of their dresses; next, followed men carrying a small rose-coloured coffin, with a white cross and white letters on it.

Friends on foot brought up the rear, with many donkeys and their drivers. I followed to see the end of the little rose-coloured coffin, and stood on a hill overlooking the Roman Catholic burial ground, into which the procession entered.

The little boys played and ran about the tombs. As soon as the rose-coloured coffin, which held the remains of their late companion, was lowered into the ground, and covered over with earth and dust, the monk, boys, and friends, all galloped back to the town.

We went one afternoon to see the French steamer, (the *Orontes*) in which we had taken a passage to Jaffa.

Arriving at the side of the vessel, we found 'coaling' going on, but when one has travelled a great deal, slight inconveniences are not much thought of, and we went on board to ascertain what accommodation the ship afforded.

It was very small. The stewardess, who was French, instantly appeared when she heard a lady was come on board. She was elderly, fat, and rather carelessly attired, but welcomed me in a most friendly manner, and seemed as if she had lived in the 'coaling' business the greater part of her life. I learnt I was to occupy the same cabin with several other ladies—besides my maid; and the stewardess added, "Pour moi je passerai la nuit à terre." This close packing though by no means agreeable, was to be borne patiently; it was only to last for a short time; and there was no remedy, so it was of no use grumbling.

Several French priests were already on board. They had over their heads white kerchiefs which hung down their backs and the sides of their faces; over these kerchiefs they had put on their hats— it was a curious head-gear certainly, but it protected them from the sun, the power of which did not seem great to us, who had recently arrived from India.

The next day, when we had got on board, the deck was crowded with people; many, however, had only come to take leave of their friends.

By degrees these visitors dropped off, and I could then see who were to be our '*compagnons de voyage.*' The ladies, especially, attracted my attention; above all, a French dame, who wore a white satin bonnet, trimmed with feathers and flowers. It seemed a curious and unusual style of bonnet for a voyage on board a steamer. The '*blacks*' which fell from the chimney of the steamer had very little respect for it, and the wearer soon disappeared into the depths below, where I found her shortly after tucked up in her berth and very unwell. Her complaints of the smallness of the vessel were vehement, and eloquent. Occasionally, she raised her little plump hands and arms into the air, displaying a pair of massive gold bracelets, and calling out "Ah quelle misère." I tried to soften her miseries by telling her they would not last long, when she exclaimed, "Ah—ah! madame, ce bel Himalaya que j'ai vu à Alexandrie; ah! quel beau vaisseau Anglais, si j'etais à bord, comme je serais heureuse, on pourrait danser sur le pont." It was so like the remark of a light-hearted Frenchwoman, but at the same time I thought it an uncommon way of making a pilgrimage to the Holy Land by *dancing* to it.

I witnessed one very comic scene. A lady, who it appears did not speak French, came into the cabin, when the stewardess, seeing she was far from well, said to her, "Madame est elle bien malade?" no answer. The stewardess spoke louder, and looking anxiously into the lady's face, exclaimed, "Ah je crains que madame ne soit très très malade," still no answer. "Ah!" cried the stewardess, "Madame ne me comprend pas— madame est—n'est ce pas?" and the Frenchwoman immediately commenced acting the '*Mal de Mer*,' to the astonishment of all the by-standers. This curious exhibition hurried me on deck again.

Dinner was soon announced, and was a contrast to that on board the steamers belonging to the East Indian Company. It is not only the 'fare,' as it is called, in these last-named steamers that is bad, but the untidiness, the want of all comfort and cleanliness, which are especially necessary to make breakfasts and dinners pleasant at sea. It will scarcely be credited that there are no stewardesses in the steamers which take passengers from Bombay to Suez. Everybody, too, must bring their own linen for the berths. It is impossible to describe all the discomforts of these steamers.[1]

There were many passengers—people from all parts of the world—some French gentlemen going to Jerusalem '*pour faire leur pâques.*' They called themselves '*Pèlerins;*' they were unshaven and unshorn. One of them was very communicative; he told me he was going with his companions on a pilgrimage to the Holy City, showing me their *future* journal, the programme of what they were to do and see each day, being already arranged! Several French priests were on board; some with sharp features, and a cunning, prying expression of countenance. Others with round, sleek, rosy cheeks, and smiling faces. Then there were English, Swiss, Australian, and French families, besides a sprinkling of gentlemen from all parts of the world, without any encumbrances at all.

How shall I describe the night? We were eight ladies in a cabin about twelve feet long and

---

[1] Since the above was written, the steamers on this line have been changed, and passengers are conveyed in boats belonging to the "Peninsular and Oriental Company," in which, I am sorry to say I learn that the accommodation is no better.

seven wide. I found, when I went below, my poor companions all more or less ill, save the French lady, who was in a tranquil state; and I hoped she might be dreaming that she was dancing on the '*bel Himalaya.*' When all was about to be shut up for the night, the stewardess made her bed on the floor (no berth could have held her, had one been unoccupied); and, when I rose in the night to get a glass of water, I had to scramble over the massive frame of the good old lady, for she and one small table completely filled the middle of the cabin.

The coast of Jaffa is very dangerous; and, as we approached it at night, we lay to till day. I was all impatience for the morning. A few passengers, as eager as myself to see the long wished-for Jaffa, were early on deck. They were lively, talkative, and anxious to communicate their feelings and thoughts to each other.

I felt that perfect quiet, and rest from the outer world, would have been more agreeable on viewing for the first time, ' Earth's most hallowed ground ' —a land, the future of which is as deeply interesting to the Christian as it is to the Jew; and where, even at this day, prophecy is no doubt being fulfilled.

It was a lovely morning—the air soft and sweet—the sky above was of a pearly, grey tint, and rather lowering. The sun was hidden behind light, motionless clouds, but very bright rays streamed down, and seemed to touch the faint outlines of the mountains, which we were to cross the next day. It was a calm, but not *triste* sky, for it seemed full of promise of a brighter day. I could not help thinking of Him who has for a time hidden His face from this once favoured country and its people; but, although their *present* is dark and lowering, they have still bright hopes for the future; for we know they will be gathered together and become once more the people of God.

The sea washes the walls of Jaffa, which stands on an eminence, the houses built close together. Here and there was a minaret, and to our left, not far from the shore, were low hills, on which grew a few small trees.

The usual confusion began when the time for landing approached. In a few minutes, heaps of boxes, bags, trunks, and portmanteaus made their appearance from below.

A stranger would have taken us for emigrants, (about to settle in the land) instead of pilgrims. Occasionally, a lady's maid would appear carrying a thin hat box, which, "of course, she had forgotten till the last moment *ought* to come," but which is detected by the quick eye of her master, who declares ' this trash' shall not go on shore—a kind word and a soft look from the mistress, however, soon set all things right. The master gives in, shrugs his shoulders, but wishes, no doubt, there were no ladies' maids in the world.

All the passengers now made their appearance. Poor sufferers crept out of their berths, and crawled down into the boat which was to convey them to the shore. There was a great swell, the boats were tossed up and down, and the passengers performed a variety of curious feats, some falling on their faces into the boat, others into the arms and laps of their companions.

The anchorage at Jaffa is very dangerous, there is no harbour, but a mere roadstead, in which no vessel could remain with the wind blowing strongly on shore; the surf rolls in with great force, and it is lucky the natives of the place are good boatmen.

In going on shore, we passed rapidly between large rocks, over which the sea was dashing with all its might, and on which it seemed impossible that the boat should not be dashed to pieces; in fine weather, however, and the wind in a favourable quarter, there is no real danger. I was not sorry to land. The streets of Jaffa are narrow and dirty. Some suppose that Jaffa derives its name from Japhet, and that he built a city here. It is frequently mentioned in the Old Testament, in the New only once, and that connected with the visit of St. Peter. The house where he lived, belonging to Simon the tanner, or rather the site of it, is pointed out; but, as we intended returning to Jaffa on leaving Jerusalem, I put off going to see it. [1]

It was at Jaffa a sad event in modern history took place. Napoleon, in 1797, caused the town to be completely and cruelly sacked. Hundreds of Turkish soldiers were taken into the neighbourhood and massacred.

We had a letter of introduction to the English Consul—a Syrian gentleman. He and his wife received us most amiably. The lady was very handsome—her costume curious, being half-European, half-Syrian. The two styles did not harmonize, in my opinion; but her beauty and sweet expression overcame the disadvantage. Her husband was extremely well-bred and pleasing, as well as striking

[1] We did not return to Jaffa—we went from Jerusalem to Beyrout—thus, I never saw the site of Simon's house —another example that we should never put off till to-morrow what we can do to-day.

in his appearance—indeed, I have found that, generally speaking, natives of the east are endowed with a high breeding altogether peculiar to them.

We must all have been very troublesome to Mr. ————. People were rushing in and out of his house, asking him to assist them in procuring horses and camels, and to protect them from the extortions of camel-drivers, &c., upon the journey to Jerusalem, as well as to do many things which were little less than impossibilities, all of which he bore with the utmost patience and good humour.

I rested for a short time in an upper room in the consul's house, overlooking the town and roadstead.

I had time to *think* a little, and to read in the Bible the different parts where Joppa is mentioned.

After breakfast our horses and camels being ready, we started for Ramlah. To my saddle hung a large strong black leather bag, containing indispensable comforts, and necessaries, among them, a map of Syria, a journal, writing and drawing materials, and several books; so that when all was packed, it was with difficulty the poor bag could close its mouth.

The gardens outside the town of Jaffa were rich in orange trees, and the odour of the various fruits and flowers was delicious. I was struck by the beauty of the women and children whom we met, their complexions were lovely, delicate, at the same time having the appearance of health; several of the children had hair of a rich chestnut colour.

We were soon on the plain of Sharon; and I thought of the verse in Can. 2. " I am the rose of Sharon, and the lily of the Valleys." Sharon is often alluded to in the old Testament.[1]

The plain over which we rode, reminded me of those in the Deccan, which I had always admired so much. Wild flowers were abundant, and at that time of the year, the road we were on was anything but a desert. It is always called, however, ' the short desert.' Every stock, stone, and briar we passed seemed to have its individual interest. I saw a great deal; but never felt that I had seen enough. Occasionally, villages were visible at a distance; near our path there was very little cultivation; olive trees and cactuses were scattered about, but the latter were not very common.

The approach to Ramlah was exceedingly pretty. The town in a bright light, looked well among the dark olive trees; and behind Ramlah rose deep rich blue hills.

[1] See 1 Chron. xxvii. 29; Isaiah xxxiii. 9; xxxv. 2; lxv. 10.

Lydda, we were told, was to our left.[1] How pleasant it would have been if we had had time to linger on our journey and visit the places near Ramlah, connected with Holy Scripture.

As we came near the town the English Consul, a Greek, met us, having heard of our expected arrival.

We saluted each other, but conversation was out of the question, he speaking no European language, we no Arabic.[2] Smiles, signs, and in fact a pantomimic proceeding were the only means we had of communicating with each other. He led us through narrow streets to his house, which he lent us for the night. One sitting room was tolerably furnished, others had neither beds, tables, nor chairs, only divans being round the rooms; but this did not signify, the camels were carrying our furniture and we were in hopes they would soon follow. They did not do so, however, for nearly four hours after our arrival; and the cook, who is a most important personage in such expeditions as this was, did not appear till a late hour. We heard that the cause of delay was a camel running away, and the baggage it carried containing part of the culinary utensils,

---

[1] See Acts ix. 32, 35, 38.

[2] Those of our servants who spoke Arabic had not yet overtaken us from Jaffa.

not being well secured, had been upset. This was our first *contre-temps.*

Shortly after our arrival, two persons made their appearance at the consul's house. One a German, the other an American. These had arrived at Ramlah with a few other of their countrymen, in order '*to spy the land,*' and ascertain whether it would be advisable to bring emigrants here from America or Germany.

It appeared that the consul had asked these two foreigners to come, being aware that they spoke English and a little Arabic; and, therefore, would be a medium of communication between himself and us. Their visit lasted so long, that, after all that could be said had been said two or three times over, I left the room, dreadfully tired, to sit in peace in the court-yard. These people followed us to re-commence the conversation. We went into another apartment; they followed. In despair, I fled to a third room, and closed the door; but they still tarried outside, talking to the gentlemen of our party. At last the consul gently hinted to the Yankee and his friend, that they would do well to return home; and we saw them no more.

The next morning I was up at a very early hour. The windows of my room looked over the plain we had traversed the day before, and the flat roofs and domes of Ramlah below the consul's house. About a quarter of a mile from the town is a white tower, situated in a grove of olive trees, and near it a Turkish burial ground. Some say this tower is part of a Christian church, others believe it to be the minaret of a mosque. I should never venture to give an opinion of what it is. One thing I do know, that it looks well in a sketch. Wise men and great travellers of the present day, are constantly disputing as to the probability or im-probability—the possibility or impossibility—of this or that place in Palestine being identical with one alluded to in Holy Writ. When a fact appears established, and the world is con-tent to believe it, a new traveller appears with some fresh theory, upsetting what were conceived to be well-founded opinions, thus Ram-lah is now said by some not to be the Arimathea of Joseph.

The view towards the east was very pretty; the plain beyond the town, over which we were to travel, looked bright and green. Many persons who visit the Holy Land do so at a time when the soil, like that of India, in the hot season, is dried up and flowerless.

In the spring of the year Palestine is beautiful. "The flowers appear on the earth, the time of the singing birds is come, and the voice of the turtle is heard in our land: the fig-tree putteth forth her green figs, and the vines with the tender grape give a good smell." [1]

Here we have not the sun of the tropics; but still it *tells*—there is no doubting that it is the sun; it looks and feels like it.

The consul came early to see us before we left Ramlah. He was much pleased at having been of service to us; accompanied us a short distance on our journey, and after we had expressed our gratitude to him for his civilities, he said ' Good-bye,' in English, returned home, and we proceeded on our journey.

The plains between Ramlah and the mountains we were about to cross, were more like those of the Deccan than even the plains of the day before. There was one purple hill resembling that on which the temple of Parbutty stands; but on these plains there were, fortunately, no altars or temples in groves, no Hunooman or Crishna, or god with five heads, four arms, and covered with red paint. The variety of wild flowers appeared to increase; but I

[1] Song of Solomon, chap. ii., verse 12, 13.

could not look long at them, for the road became so
bad and rocky, I had to attend to my horse's feet,
and think of my own safety.

At the foot of the mountains, the Vale of Sharon
terminates. Now we began to ascend, the roads
became worse every minute; but the horses were
accustomed to them, and they carried us up and
down rocks, over rolling stones, and slippery paths
with the greatest composure. I was told by my companions to "consider myself a sack of potatoes,
and all would go right." I strictly obeyed orders,
and I very soon became quite courageous, though
the mountain-paths up and down which we rode
were, I am assured, bad enough to shake the
strongest nerves. The hills were, generally speaking, barren—here and there patches of cultivation,
and a great deal of low underwood, bearing a
yellow flower like that of the broom in England:
but the impression of the surrounding scenery was
that of desolation. We passed, by mistake, the
place where travellers usually dismount and rest,
continuing to toil up and down the rocky hills and
ravines till we reached an open space of ground
much more than half way to Jerusalem, where we
got off our horses, and found the wine, water, and
biscuits, which we had with us, most acceptable, for
we had ridden for four hours.

The next place of interest we passed was Karyet-el-Enab, which great authorities identify with the Kirjeth-Baal or Kirjeth-Jearim (City of forests), often mentioned in the Old Testament. The village situated on the side of a hill is a wild, desolate-looking place. Formerly it belonged entirely to hereditary freebooters, known by the name of Abu-Ghosh, who rendered the journey to Jerusalem extremely dangerous. It is only a few years since the principal actor in many daring attacks on travellers, was taken and executed, I believe, by order of Ibrahim Pacha. The road can now be passed with perfect safety.

It will be remembered that the ark of the covenant was carried there from Bethshemesh when rescued from the Philistines.[1] There is an old Latin church at Kirjeth-Baal. I believe it is in ruins, but we did not go to see it; if we had had time to do so, I do not know if I should have had strength, I was already much fatigued.

As we toiled on our way hoping at every turn of the road (if road it could be called, for there was scarcely a trace of a path-way), to see Jerusalem,

---

[1] 'And it came to pass while the ark abode in Kirjath-Jearim, that the time was long, for it was twenty years; and all the house of Israel lamented after the Lord.'— 1 Sam. vii. 2.

we met gaunt, clumsy camels, which always seem to come sprawling along, placing their long graceless legs anywhere and everywhere, and as they never get out of the way for anybody, it is difficult sometimes, in a narrow place, to avoid a collision, which would be far from pleasant, as the burdens and baggage they carry (frequently hanging far over their sides), threaten the traveller with a broken or, at least, a bruised, leg or arm.

As we approached Jerusalem, the cultivation became less and less. There were occasional vineyards, but olive trees were fewer; the wild flowers continued plentiful, their brilliant colours rendering the surrounding barrenness still more striking. This partial cultivation of the land brought to my mind the fourth and sixth verses of the seventeenth chapter of Isaiah. "And in that day it shall come to pass, that the glory of Jacob shall be made thin, and the fatness of his flesh shall wax lean. Yet, gleaming grapes shall be left in it, as the shaking of an olive tree, two or three berries in the top of the uttermost bough, four or five in the outmost fruitful branches thereof, saith the Lord God of Israel."

When the journey was drawing to a close, we met the Bishop of Jerusalem and Mrs. Gobat, who kindly rode out from Jerusalem to greet us; and from them we heard we were about two miles from the city. There was much to observe, our friends pointing out different sites where deeply-interesting events, spoken of in Biblical history, took place.

On our nearer approach to Jerusalem, we saw, in the extreme distance, the mountains of Ammon and Moab; and the beautiful story of Ruth, the Moabitess, was instantly present to my mind. The village, or rather town, of Bethlehem was to our right, situated on a high hill. Further on, the convent of Elias, or Elijah, was pointed out to us, and a Greek church, where tradition asserts the tree of the wood of which the cross was made, grew. Presently the Mount of Olives rose before us. We felt all around was so real—so solemn. The feelings with which we approached all these localities were quite different from any that had been excited in us on first seeing other parts of the world, however interesting they might be. I am sure *all* have experienced this on visiting Jerusalem, however they might differ whether this or that place be the one mentioned in the Old or New Testament. No one doubts it is holy ground—that it *is* Bethlehem, that it *is* the Mount of Olives; for although we are all aware that

> "Thy footsteps all in Sion's deep decay,
>   Were blotted from the holy ground; yet dear
>   Is every stone of hers; for Thou wast surely there."[1]

I was so fatigued, I wonder I saw anything. We had been eight hours on the journey. We approached Jerusalem on the western side: the walls crown the brow of the hill, and the buildings of the Armenian quarter were visible above the walls.

We were a large party, and entered the Jaffa Gate somewhat in confusion and bustle, the tired horses slipping over a very rough pavement. Passing a small dirty bazaar, we reached the hotel, situated in a very narrow street, where apartments had already been engaged for us through the kindness of the excellent bishop.

[1] Keble's 'Christian Year.'   Monday before Easter.

CHAPTER VIII.

THE first sounds I heard early in the morning the day after my arrival at Jerusalem, were a discordant Turkish band, next the bells of an adjacent convent, and then the voices of children joining in a hymn. They were already in the school belonging to one of the Christian churches.

The window of my room looked over a pool, formerly supposed to be the pool of Hezekiah, and the one spoken of in Isaiah, xxii. 9., 2 Chron. xxxii. 3, 4 ;

but two great authorities, Messrs. Williams and
Robinson, differ on this subject, the latter ascrib-
ing it to Hezekiah, the former believing it to be
the Almond Pool, mentioned by Josephus in his
account of the Siege of Jerusalem by Titus. The
dimensions of this pool are about two hundred and
forty feet by one hundred and forty four.[1] It is in
the Christian quarter, and entirely surrounded by
buildings. At one of the corners a flight of steps
leads down to the water, which washes the very
walls of the houses.

Our first walk was down the Via Dolorosa,
which leads to St. Stephen's gate.

The pavement in the streets is very bad, and
the donkey I rode, though accustomed to it, was
constantly tripping.

Several objects of interest were shown us by our
guide, an old Christian Arab, called Thomas, such
as a stone in a wall, which our Lord touched as he
went through this street to the hall of judgment,
then a stone pillar, nearly sunk in the ground, and
where He is said to have rested. We passed
under an archway, where it is supposed that Pilate
showed our Lord to the people; it is called,
therefore, the arch of 'Ecce Homo.'

[1] Robinson's Biblical Researches, page 487.

These traditions are devoutly believed in by the Latin, Greek, and other eastern churches here. The wish of the monks in early times to prove too much has done a great deal of mischief; and many persons, finding it impossible to believe all, doubt even what would seem to be reasonable evidence in relation to places that are pointed out as the spots where certain events narrated in the Bible took place. I always thought those happier who believed too much, than those who believed *only a little.*

Near St. Stephen's gate (called by the natives Mary's gate) is the pool of Bethesda, where the sheep market [1] was situated; and from the gate itself there is a road leading down to the valley of Jehoshaphat, at the bottom of which runs the brook Kedron; a little further on is the garden of Gethsemane; immediately above which the Mount of Olives suddenly rises.

We stopped some little time looking at the scene around us. In the distance to the right were the mountains of Moab, their summits fading away into the soft blue evening sky. Near us and close to the city walls was a Turkish cemetery, where many Mahomedan women were standing or sitting, veiled from head to foot; they had come to pay their

[1] St. John v. 2.

weekly visit to the tombs of their relations. When at Cairo I used to see the Arabs carrying branches of palms every Friday, when they performed this duty.

As the evening was far advanced, and the gates of the town are always closed at sunset, we did not descend into the valley.

One morning I went on a donkey to St. Stephen's gate, dismounted, and sat for some time on the platform which overlooks the valley below. The sun had already risen over the Mount of Olives, and the sky was cloudless. The distant mountains, the nearer hills and valleys, had their histories both in the Old and New Testament; and it was impossible to say which was uppermost in my thoughts, the past or future of the place. I read the fourteenth chapter of Zechariah while I remained here, and could scarcely think the fourth verse is to be taken in a figurative sense, though I have heard persons say it ought to be so understood. The coming of Christ is spoken of in these words, "And his feet shall stand in that day upon the Mount of Olives, which is before Jerusalem in the east, and the Mount of Olives shall cleave in the midst thereof towards the east and towards the west, and there shall be a very great valley; and half of the mountain shall remove toward the north and half of it toward the south."

On my right, but inside the walls, was the site of the temple; this place is now occupied by the great mosque.

Descending into the Valley of Jehoshaphat, I passed by the brook of Kedron. This brook is alluded to in the 2 Samuel, xv. 23; also in St. John, xviii. 1. There is scarcely any water in it at this time of year, but I found several pretty flowers on its banks which I gathered and endeavoured to dry on my return to the hotel. Beyond the brook a Greek church, in which the tomb said to be that of the Virgin is shewn, has been built many feet below the level of the road. Several lovely children were playing at the entrance, waiting for their parents who had gone into the church for their morning devotions. They were joyous, laughing little creatures, gathering and playing with beautiful flowers, and the scene brought to my mind those lines of Mr. Lisle Bowles.

> " When summer comes, the little children play
> In the churchyard of our cathedral grey,
> Busy as morning bees, and gathering flowers
> In the brief sunshine ; they of coming hours
> Reck not, intent upon their play though time
> Speed like a spectre by them, and their prime
> Bear on to sorrow."

A broad flight of steps leads down into this church, on one side of which the tombs of Anna (the mother of the Virgin Mary) and Joseph are supposed to be. Several women enveloped in white mantles passed before me. I remained behind looking at the strange scene beneath me, the mass of white drapery standing well out in the deep shadows around it. As the women did not go into the body of the church, I remained with them, and as I sat on the steps, heard the priests chanting; for a short time I could distinguish nothing but a few lights glimmering below, presently I could perceive many lamps suspended from the ceiling, but the few that were burning, only threw a dim light on the figures in black; sometimes I could distinguish a distinct form, but generally it was a mass of black. All around me were women in white, some standing, some kneeling, some "making conversation," others quieting crying babies, while little merry children kept running after each other up and down the steps.

As I returned to the hotel, I stayed some little time at the Pool of Bethesda. It is, or rather was (for it is now dry), on the left of St. Stephen's gate (as I returned from the Valley of Jehoshaphat), and close to Mount Moriah, where stood the Temple of Solomon. The Mosque of Omar—'the Noble Sanctuary,' as it is called by the Mahomedans—now stands on Mount Moriah.

The Pool of Bethesda is surrounded by buildings on three sides; on the east side, where I sat, is a very low ruinous wall, with wild flowers growing all over it. The pool is very deep—nothing in it but large mounds of green turf; the only appearance of water was that of a scanty stream trickling out from a wall, belonging to a Turkish public bath. This spot is, indeed, one of the 'waste places' of Jerusalem, and reminded me of Ezekiel vii. 21., where he speaks of the future desolation of Israel:—"And I will give it into the hands of the stranger for a prey, and to the wicked of the earth for a spoil, and they shall pollute it."

Some doubt whether this is the Pool of Bethesda spoken of in the Gospel; but Mr. Williams, author of 'The Holy City,' is of opinion that it is the pool.

The site of Pontius Pilate's house is on the left-hand side of the Via Dolorosa, returning from the gate, and is now occupied by a barrack. When I arrived, a Turkish officer went up with me to the flat roof, in order that I might see the prospect, and the mosque built on Mount Moriah. None but

true believers are allowed to enter the sacred en-
closure; but I had a very good idea of the whole
from the elevated position I occupied, which commanded a view of all the buildings on the mount.
Behind the large mosque, to the south, is a smaller
one—that of El Aksa; and outside the wall of this
sanctuary is the wailing-place of the Jews.   The
space occupied by these two mosques is very extensive, and planted with cypress and olive-trees.
In the eastern wall which encloses it is the Golden-
Gate, now walled up.   From where I stood, I could
see (rather to the right) the Hill of Evil Counsel
the Tower of Hippicus, and the Church of the Holy
Sepulchre.

The hotel we lived in was full of people from
nearly every country.   There were German counts,
French Priests, and barons.   Americans and Englishmen of all professions, from Australia, China, and
India.   The topics of conversation in a society so
mixed, were, it my be easily imagined, very
various, and there was often much said that was
calculated to instruct, and not a little that surprised and amused.

A Frenchman speaking of his visit to Jerusalem,
said, " il n'y a pas de promenade ici," missing his
" Bois de Boulogne," and his cafés!   Another en-

lightened individual who had just returned from the Antipodes, said he " saw nothing at the Dead Sea worthy of a visit." Some were all enthusiasm, seeing with the eyes of their minds as well as those of their bodies. Let the reader fancy one of these enthusiasts sitting by a sedate, quiet gentleman at the table d'hote, and on narrating all he had seen that morning with the greatest animation, receiving for reply, " Well sir, you think you have seen the tomb of the Virgin Mary, now sir, you have seen no such thing! From undoubted authority, it is known not to exist."

The poor crest-fallen enthusiast retorts by re-marking to the other—he probably does not believe he is at Jerusalem.

" Yes sir, I am perfectly aware I am at Jerusalem, but let us talk no more on the subject."

We visited the school for Jewish and Arab children, which is under the superintendence of the Protestant bishop. There were but few little Jewesses there, as it was Friday, and Friday is ' the wailing day.' Among the children in the school, very few had been baptized. They learn reading, writing, arithmetic and ' plain work.' The Jewesses were mostly fair, rosy-cheeked, and many had auburn hair. It is a pity they do not retain more of their national dress. The boys struck me as being very intelligent, and one little fellow explained a proposition in Euclid, I was told, very well. He was an Arab, with a bright and pleasing countenance.

The wailing of the Jews, I have said, takes place every Friday.

We passed through a very dirty bazaar and several miserable streets, in order to get to the wailing-place. The dirt in the streets in this Jewish quarter surpassed even that at Cairo. The stones of the pavement are of every form and size—some pointed, others loose and rolling—when you think you are on a stone firmly fixed in the ground, it turns round, and you find yourself stumbling and tumbling about in all directions. Even the donkeys one rides are often on their noses, and the poor beasts are chastised because the roads are bad.

The spot were the Jews assemble is small, and very narrow, situated behind the high wall which encloses the 'noble sanctuary.' Antiquarians say that some part of the masonry of the high wall, against which the people turn their faces and wail, is as old as the time of Solomon. This wailing is one of the 'sights' of Jerusalem; but, when there, I thought it rather an odd amusement to go and stare at a number of people lamenting over the sorrows of their country; and, although some of them may resort there from habit, no doubt there were others who really felt that, " Judah is gone into captivity, because of affliction, and because of great servitude; she dwelleth among the heathen; she findeth no rest; all her persecutors overtook her between the straits." [1]

When we arrived at the place, we found several Jews and a few Jewesses with their faces turned towards the wall. Some reading out of large, dirty books. I only heard one Jew 'wailing.' They turned round, looked at us, and seemed *to say*, " Is it nothing to you, all ye that pass by? behold and see if there be any sorrow like unto my sorrow which is done unto me, wherewith the Lord has afflicted me in his fierce anger." [2]

It was a sight one could not see unmoved, and as the poor people again turned towards the wall I felt how true it is that " He hath violently taken away His tabernacle, as if it were of a garden, He hath destroyed the places of His assembly." [3]

One of the Jews there, who was a German, showed us his book; he was reading the Psalms of

[1] Lamentations of Jeremiah, i. 3.
[2] *Ibid.* i. 12. [3] *Ibid.* ii. 6.

David. The top of the page was in Hebrew; the translation of the Psalm and the commentary were in German, but in the Hebrew character.

The first visit I paid to the church of the Holy Sepulchre was with several people. 'Sight-seeing,' in company is never agreeable, unless there be a strong sympathy in taste and feeling. I felt this more particularly at Jerusalem. I returned to the hotel with a very confused idea of what I had seen.

During my stay in Jerusalem I was often able to go to the Church of the Sepulchre alone. I, one day, made a long visit and saw nearly every thing. Almost the first object of interest pointed out to the stranger is a long marble slab on the pavement like a tombstone. At each end were three very large candlesticks covered with red velvet. At this spot it is said our Saviour was anointed for His burial. People were prostrating themselves on the slab and kissing it. To the left, not far off, is shown the place where the Virgin stood while the body was anointed. On the right are the tombs of Godfrey de Bouillon, of Baldwin the first, and Melchisedech, and the small chapel of St. Iohn the Baptist, and Adam.

There is a grating in the wall of this chapel, where a fissure in the rock is shown which was formed when the 'rocks were rent,' at the crucifixion of our Lord. The traditions connected with this church of the Holy Sepulchre are so many that I must pass them by, for they would occupy an entire chapter.

The chapel of St. John the Baptist and Adam, that of Godfrey de Bouillon and Baldwin the First,[1] are, with the chapels of the crucifixion and exaltation of the cross, frequently called the chapels of Calvary. A staircase leads up to the chapels of the crucifixion and exaltation of the cross. These are much ornamented; there are two altars, one belonging to the Greeks, and the other to the Latins. I then descended into the rotunda, where stands the Holy Sepulchre. It is twenty-six feet in length, and eighteen broad. It is built of a yellowish marble, and countless silver lamps are suspended over the entrance, which is adorned by three large enamelled medallions, the frame of the middle one being enriched with coloured stones, which are said to be real. The doorway is elaborately

[1] Though the tombs of Godfrey de Bouillon and Baldwin the First are still pointed out, Mr. Williams, in his 'Holy City,' tells us that these sepulchral monuments were defaced and injured by the Charizmians, in 1244; and by the Greeks, because they commemorated Latin sovereigns; and it seems that, in the late restoration, they have been wholly destroyed and obliterated from a similar motive.

carved. There are two divisions in the building; the first you enter is called the 'Chapel of the Angel,' and is very small: in the middle is a marble monument, which looks much like a font; it is said to mark the place where the stone was rolled from the door of the sepulchre, and where the angel was seen sitting. Many persons came in while I was there to kiss this monument, some kneeling and continuing absorbed in prayer for a minute or two. From this small room you enter where the sepulchre is believed to have been.

The ornaments of the entrance to this room are beautifully and richly carved. Each of these divisions is so small that not more than four persons can be in it together. A shelf placed against the wall was arranged as an altar, on which stood lighted candles and vases of flowers. Over the slab which marks the spot where the body of our Saviour was placed, hung many gilt lamps—a few lighted; on the wall were three pictures—one belonging to the Latins, one to the Greeks, and one to the Armenians. While I was in the sepulchre, a Greek priest was reading, and occasionally occupied in meditating; he had a small silver bottle full of rose-water, with which he sometimes sprinkled the flowers on the altar, from whence he gave me lavender and wall-flowers. The entrance to the Greek church is directly opposite the Holy Sepulchre. This church is large, and much decorated.

The spots where our Saviour appeared to Mary Magdalene and to His mother, are marked by small round marble slabs in the pavement, not far from the Latin chapel,[1] which is plain in its ornaments. In the Church of the Holy Sepulchre, are several small side-chapels; among them—that of St. Mary; of Longinus, the Centurion; ' of the parting of our Lord's garments;' and one where is shown a stone, on which it is said our Saviour sat when he was mocked.

The Copts have only one altar in the church; it is placed close behind the sepulchre of our Lord. The Syrians have a small, unfurnished chapel, in which are the tombs where Joseph of Arimathea, and Nicodemus, are said to have been buried.

In St. Helena's Chapel, which belongs to the Greeks, a small window is shown, from whence the empress watched the workmen below, and urged them on in their endeavours to discover the three crosses; and an altar now marks the spot where tradition says they were found.

The Armenian chapel contains curious pictures;

[1] Called also ' the Chapel of the Apparition.'

one of the Virgin, round her neck is a chain of gold coins. Another picture represents our Lord ascending from the Mount of Olives—he ascends into clouds gilt over; behind them rise the heads of angels who are blowing trumpets; and on the spot from whence our Saviour has ascended are two very large foot marks.

The roof of the rotunda in which the sepulchre stands was in bad repair when we were at Jerusalem. The Greek and Latin churches had, I understood, disputed with whom the right to put it in order rested, and while this discussion went on, the roof became more dilapidated, so much so that the rain came in, and the altar belonging to the Copts was in danger of being materially injured.

I have not entered into detail in describing each and every deeply interesting object in the Church of the Holy Sepulchre. Details would be tedious to many persons, and I have therefore given only a *rough sketch* of what is there to be seen.

One afternoon was occupied in walking round Jerusalem. Passing out of St. Stephen's gate and descending the Valley of Jehoshaphat we saw on the left hand side a grotto arranged as a chapel in which were two small plain altars, and then we entered the garden of Gethsemane. How true is the remark of Dr. Wilson in his " Lands of the Bible," that

Gethsemane " is a place, the associations of which are of overwhelming interest and solemnity." We read that not far from it our blessed Lord went forward a little, and fell on the ground, and prayed, saying those memorable words, " not my will but thine be done,"[1] which have been perhaps of all those uttered by Him the most comforting and soothing for countless mourning Christians, and will continue to be so till He shall swallow up death " in victory, and the Lord God shall wipe tears from off all faces."

The garden is small, enclosed by high walls. I regret that it has been converted into a modern garden ; the flowers are, however, pretty. There are neat terrace walks, and a few ancient olive trees. A Spanish lady, who visited this garden, had small paintings let into the wall, representing the various events which took place during our Lord's sojourn on earth.

We now ascended the Mount of Olives, which is mentioned in the 2 Samuel, xv. 30., as connected

---

[1] The reader will remember those beautiful lines of Keble—
"' O Father ! not My will, but Thine be done.'
So spake the Son.
Be this our charm, mellowing earth's ruder noise
Of griefs and joys ;
That we may cling for ever to Thy breast
In perfect rest !"
The Christian Year—Wednesday before Easter.

with the history of David and Absalom, when the former fled from Jerusalem. It is often read of in the gospels, and was a favourite resort of our Saviour. All the walks about Jerusalem must be traversed with reverential feelings; but the garden of Gethsemane, the Mount of Olives, and Bethany, have a peculiar interest.

The path leading up the Mount is steep and stony. Olive trees are pretty numerous in all directions, and are peculiarly suited to the scenery around Jerusalem. They have an air of sadness and gloom with their sombre trunks and dark green leaves; and they seem in mourning for the sorrows of the land and its people.

When we reached the summit of the hill it was so windy and cold, we could not look at the views with any comfort. Turning to the west, the entire city of Jerusalem is seen completely walled in. The present wall was raised by Suliman the first. The date, 1541-2, is to be seen in some parts of the wall. From the top of the Mount, one has a bird's-eye view of the city. Towards the south-east, the mountains of Moab and the Dead Sea were visible.

It has been the received opinion for ages, and is still universally believed, that the Saviour's ascension took place from the Mount of Olives. Although I am most willing to cling to all the ancient traditions, if I may venture to state an opinion in which others more competent to judge than I am agree with me, I think that event occurred at Bethany, and not at the Mount of Olives, as it is clearly stated in the twenty-fourth chapter of St. Luke, 50, 51 verses, that " He led them out *as far as to Bethany*, and He lifted up His hands and blessed them; and it came to pass while He blessed them He was parted from them, and carried up into Heaven."

Inside the church, which crowns the summit of the Mount, is a large stone, marking the spot from whence it is believed our Lord's ascent took place.

Descending the hill we passed two places, at one of which we are told our Saviour taught his disciples the Lord's Prayer; and at the other, the Apostles made the creed. I could not help fearing these assertions were apocryphal. Further on are some curious grottoes, said to be the burial-place of the prophets. In the valley of Jehoshaphat and Hinnom, through which we rode this evening, there are tombs and graves, both ancient and modern, in every direction. It is impossible to pass by the numerous grottoes and burying-places without thinking that perhaps out of some of them, " many bodies of saints arose, and came out of the graves after His resurrection, and went into the Holy City, and appeared unto many."

That chapter of Ezekiel wherein we read— "And He said unto me, Son of man, can these bones live? and I answered, O Lord God thou knowest," [1] recurred to my mind. Nor could I help recalling these striking words. "I will also gather all nations, and will bring them down into the valley of Jehoshaphat, and I will plead with them for my people, and for my heritage Israel, whom they have scattered among the nations, and parted my land." [2]

To our right was a tomb where Absalom is said to have been interred. [3] I observed as I passed a great quantity of stones heaped up against it. On enquiry, I heard it was usual for all who passed the tomb to throw a stone at it. The valley here is wild and pretty; there are many olive trees. The tombs of St. James and Zachariah are not far distant from that of Absalom.

The next interesting object is the Fountain of the Virgin. We then arrive at the Pool of Siloam: this is a very picturesque spot. The walls on each side nearly hidden by plants, creepers, and trailing

1 Ezekiel xxxvii. 3.   2 Joel iii. 2.

3 He was we are told buried in a large pit in the wood of Ephraim, and stones heaped upon him.

leaves and flowers. The village of Siloam is situated on a height opposite the pool, overlooking the Valley of Jehoshaphat. In Nehemiah iii. 15, and in John ix. 7, this pool is mentioned.

We next saw the Fountain of En-rogel, where, it will be remembered, Adonijah, after he had praclaimed himself king, 'slew sheep, and oxen, and fat cattle,'[1]

The Field of Blood is on a hill above the Valley of Hinnom. It was formerly usual to throw the bodies of pilgrims who died at Jerusalem into a pit, which is still seen on the Field of Blood.

Continuing our excursion through the Valley of Hinnom, we passed the lower Pool of Gihon, the Jaffa gate on the west, then the Damascus gate on the north side of the walls. To our left was the way to the Grotto of Jeremiah; further on we passed Herod's Gate (now walled up), and turning round to the eastern wall, found ourselves again at the spot from whence we had started, having made a complete tour of the city.

Another day we went to see the Armenian church situated in the Christian quarter, its ornaments are very gaudy, and by no means handsome. The wainscoting of the walls to the height of a few feet was of coloured tiles. The Armenian Patriarch has built a palace for himself.

[1] 1 Kings i. 9.

We went to pay him a visit, and found him in a large, handsome, and lofty room; he was a very fine tall old gentleman, with a long grey beard, and had on a flowing dark coloured robe, and a purple velvet cap. His manners were very pleasing. I was over-fatigued and not well, and as among our party present at this visit, there were several who talked well at all times, and who now kept up a sufficiently animated conversation with the Patriarch, I sat still and said nothing. The old man remarking my silence, explained to me, through an interpreter, that he thought it odd I said nothing. It is a pretty general feeling that when one is ' told to talk,' one cannot. I was much amused when he added:—" It would be better to say anything than to say nothing at all." This well merited reprimand, however, did not mend matters, nor endow me with the gift of speech. As the visit was too long, I welcomed the appearance of pipes, and coffee— which in Egypt and Syria, correspond to betel-nut, otto of rose, and sweetmeats at a durbar in India, the appearence of these things is a very polite hint that it is time to retire. Before we left, the Patriarch sent for a print of the queen which he was anxious to shew us. It was a very indifferent coloured one; but he was much delighted with it.

CHAPTER IX.

THE Tower of Hippicus, which stands on the Holy hill of Zion, is well worth a visit. This tower shares the fate of many things at Jerusalem, its origin being doubted and disputed, some affirming it to be *the* tower erected by King Herod, while others hold the contrary; but as wiser heads than mine cannot settle the point, it would be unbecoming in me to venture an opinion. All, however, agree that the masonry of the lower part is extremely ancient.

The prospect from the summit of the tower is very extensive. As we looked on the Mount of Olives, towards the east the mountains beyond the

Dead Sea were visible. To the north-east, was the Quarantana wilderness, the supposed locality of our Lord's temptation, as also the road to Anathoth, the birth-place and residence of the Prophet Jeremiah. [1]

On the south, was the road to Bethlehem, on the north, that to Bethel, and on the west, that to Jaffa.

Not far from the town are the Hill of Evil Council, and the Mount of Offence. On the former, tradition tells us, stood the country-house of Caiaphas, in which Judas concluded his bargain to betray the Saviour. The Mount of Offence is so called, as it is the supposed site of the abominations of Solomon's idolatry. [2]

The Tomb of David, and the town-house of Caphius, the high-priest, near the Zion gate, are to the south. Immediately below us, glittering in the sun, were the principal buildings of the city.

We looked on the English church, and on the Syrian and Armenian convents. Further off we

---

[1] Joshua xx. 18.

[2] " Then did Solomon build a high place for Chemosh, the abomination of Moab, in the hill that is before Jerusalem, and for Molech, the abomination of the children of Ammon."— 1 Kings xi. 7.

saw the church of the Holy Sepulchre, Coptic and Greek convents, and the mosque on Mount Moriah.

This panoramic view embraces more interesting localities and objects, than, perhaps, any other in the world, although there certainly is not any beautiful scenery. All around, the landscape gives one the impression of desolation and decay, and in the contemplation of it, there was enough to remind one, "that the cities of Judah should be desolate, and that gladness and joy should be taken out of the plentiful fields."

Our departure for the Dead Sea and Jericho being determined on, we left Jerusalem on the seventh of March, 1854. When we arrived at the Jaffa gate, we found a crowd who had come out to see the strangers leave. The sheikh and his guard who were to protect us on our journey greeted us most cordially; women, children, beggars of all kinds, the blind, the halt and the maimed were calling out for "Backshish," camels laden and unladen were standing and lying on the ground; mules and horses covered with baggage were ready to start: the muleteers wrangling among themselves seemed to forget everything but their own quarrels, and were only brought to order by the head muleteer rushing among them and dispersing them to the right and left. We had a litter which was in fact much like a palanquin in form, a mule being harnessed between poles both before and behind, and a man always walking beside the leading one.

When all was ready I entered the litter and we began our march. I had not gone far before I discovered I could see nothing in my place of confinement, I therefore got upon my horse which was ready, and with which I soon became acquainted. Turning to the left on leaving the Jaffa gate we went to the Valley of Hinnom. Just after we left Bethany we passed the valley where the sheikh and his companions lived; here they were met by men bringing their guns. Our Arabs were fine-looking men, some with handsome features—their dress picturesque. Besides guns they had swords and axes—they were in high spirits, and as we proceeded on our way they climbed up and ran down the heights like goats; they gathered flowers for me, and gave us some of their bread to eat. The latter act was a token of their complete friendship for us—and that we were under their protection.

We intended to reach the convent of Saint Saba by sunset, therefore we made the best of our way, the road, or rather track, being so bad, that we went at a foot's pace all the time. We passed over rocky heights, and descended into stony wadys (valleys)—now and then catching a glimpse of the Dead Sea.

The wildness and loneliness of the scene were very striking, a tree was rarely to be seen, only sometimes a low bush; no village; scarcely a human being. We rode by one Arab encampment, the tents as "black as Kedar." Wild barking dogs ran out—women and children as wild-looking as the dogs peeped at us, half frightened, and seemed glad when we had ridden by—now and then, at a distance, we saw a camel plodding along with its lazy, unconcerned step, on its back an Arab rocking to and fro with the ends of his yellow and red kerchief floating in the breeze, and the tip of his· spear glistening in the setting sun.

The scenery as we came near to the Greek convent of Saint Saba, became wilder, grander. The roads wind round a hill; a low stone wall runs along the precipitous edge of a deep ravine, in which the brook Kedron flows later in the year. The bottom of the ravine was dry, and the heaps of stones and rocks in it looked like those in a nullah (bed of a river) in India, just before the rains. On the other side of this very steep ravine, rose terraces of rocks, on which scarcely a symptom of

herbage was distinguishable, there being but a few
wild flowers; the place was even too gloomy for *them*.
In the walls of rock on the other side of the ravine,
were numerous grottoes, once the abode of ascetics;
I scarcely think they could have found a more retired
spot for meditation. Here there was certainly but
little to distract them.

We soon came in sight of the convent. It is
built on a rock, and some part of the building extends down the sides of the stony hill; below, is
the dried-up bed of the brook Kedron. A short
distance from the convent are two towers; in one,
European ladies receive accommodation when they
travel without tents—gentlemen being taken into
the convent.

I hear that, when ladies are to pass the night in
the tower, they have to climb a ladder, as there
are no steps, to a door which is placed at an unusual height from the ground; and, in fact, it
looks more like a window than a door. Having
tents, I and my maid were not doomed to scramble
up the ladder and be shut up in that prison-like
looking tower.

Behind Saint Saba were hills and barren rocks.

The tents were pitched in a ravine, not far from
the two towers, and from whence we had a view of
the mountains of Moab.

As soon as I dismounted, I went to sketch at a short distance from the convent. It was a remarkable view, and the colouring entirely 'neutral tint.' The sky iron-grey, and a line of cold, lifeless light, neither white nor grey, separating the sky from ranges of gloomy, desolate hills, and dark, barren rocks; the white buildings of the convent standing well out against the surrounding bleak and wild landscape. There was no tree; the foreground was all rock, with a few scanty, ill-grown bushes, and weeds growing here and there. This was the picture I had before me; it was certainly peculiar, and unlike any view I had ever seen before. Two of the Arabs went with me to the place from whence I wished to take this sketch. When I had finished, a gentleman of our party determined to walk a short distance alone. I begged him to take one of the guard with him; but thinking no evil could befal him if he went only a little way from the tents, he declined doing so. In half an hour he returned, saying that, having gone further than he intended, he had been overtaken by two Arabs, whose manner was evidently not friendly. Fortunately some European travellers came up, and the men, seeing he would be protected, ran off, and were soon out of sight. This road, which leads to Jericho, has always been regarded as unsafe at times. It will be remembered that the incidents related in the parable of the Good Samaritan took place between Jerusalem and Jericho.

St. Saba, to whom the church is dedicated, was born, it is supposed, in the year 439: his sepulchre is shown inside the church, I understand; though it is believed the body was removed to Venice.

Just before I had retired to my tent for the night, I saw our Arabs preparing for their evening devotions. They stood in a half circle; one man standing in front acted as leader of the ceremonies. For a little time they merely repeated some words or sentences, occasionally clapping their hands. Then they all advanced a few steps, and commenced swinging their bodies backwards and forwards, like the dervishes, repeating continually 'Mahomeda, Mahomeda,' the clapping of their hands becoming more frequent.

The next morning we were all up betimes. The night was not very quiet. The Arabs would talk, the horses would neigh, and one might as well have hoped to have prevented the latter from neighing, as the former from talking.

The scenery from the convent of St. Saba to the Dead Sea had much the same character as that we had passed through the day before.

After toiling over steep hills, and down rocky rugged paths for about three hours, we approached the 'sea of the plain.'[1]   About a mile from it, there was a remarkable change in the soil, the wild flowers had disappeared, bushes looked sad and sorry, stunted trees, and long grass, dried brambles and briars became common.

We dismounted on the beach, and rested for half an hour.   The scenery, I have heard described as ' lovely.'   There is no loveliness I think—it is solemn—grand—stern.

The day was favourable, for it was very sombre, dull and cloudy.   I should think a sunny day would not suit the place.

In the extreme distance there was a deep shadow, which struck across the water; to the left were the rocky hills of Moab, that seem to touch the water's edge; to the right the hills we had just passed over. The sea, of course, much of the same colour as the sky; there was not a breath of wind, occasionally, a ripple, and then a small wave broke up against the shore on which we sat.   The beach was stony,

[1] Deuteronomy iv. 49.

on it were many shells, a few small flowering weeds
peeping through the poor soil, and trunks of trees
strewn about, brought down by the river Jordan,
which runs into the Dead Sea. Of course we
tasted the water; it was very disagreeable, and our
hands, after being dipped in it, remained for a long
time encrusted with salt. This East Sea, as it is
called in Ezekiel xlvii. 18, is not once alluded to in
the Gospels.

Sodom and Gomorrah are believed to have been
on the east, and Zoar (to which city Lot fled) on
the west of it. We were, however, very far from
that part where it is said these cities were situated.
After the destruction of Sodom and Gomorrah,
the Dead Sea is again mentioned in Zachariah
xiv. 8, as "the former sea." Its length is about
thirty-nine miles, and its utmost breadth from nine
to ten miles.

After a short halt, we recommenced our journey
to Jericho, the way leading over a brown, poor, un-
cultivated plain, and the few low bushes we met
with, looked blighted and shrivelled. Such is now
part of the plain so pleasant in the eyes of Lot,
which he chose for his residence when he parted
from Abraham.

The River Jordan was to our right. We soon

neared its banks. Reeds and low bushes grew close to the water, which was very muddy. The stream was extremely strong, gushing over rocks and stones.

At that part of the river where it is said our Lord was baptized, we got off our horses. Pilgrims immerse themselves here in the holy stream; this is not always done with decorum, as they frequently amuse themselves by throwing the water over each other.

The banks are thickly wooded; willows, seemingly being very abundant. The sudden change from a plain evidently wasted and blasted, to wooded banks and graceful trees, with their boughs bending over the stream, was not only striking, but very pleasing. We remained a little time, in order that I might take a sketch of the scene before us; it was pretty; and, though somewhat wild, it was not unlike a home-bit, such as one often meets with in England.

Independent of the various reflections which arise when one recalls to mind, on the spot, the short and simple narrative of the baptism of Jesus, in the 3rd chapter of St. Matthew's Gospel, one of the most remarkable incidents mentioned in Holy Writ is here brought before us in the separate

manifestation of the three persons of the Holy
Trinity. We read, that the voice of God was
heard, the descent of the Holy Ghost was witnessed
in the form of a dove, and the Son of God seen
going straightway out of the water.

Before leaving, we drank some of the water; it
had no peculiar taste; and we took none away with
us in bottles, as is usually done, for it would have been
hopeless to have attempted to bring it in safety to
England, since we intended to go as far as Damascus
and Beyrout, and therefore had a long journey before us.

We approached the site of Jericho, towards sunset,
through a few cultivated fields; still what Keble
says is true—

> "Where is the land with milk and honey flowing,
>   The promise of our God, our fancy's theme?
> Here over shattered walls dark weeds are growing,
>   And blood and fire have run in mingled stream.
> Like oaks and cedars all around,
> The giant corses strew the ground,
> And haughty Jericho's cloud piercing wall,
> Lies where it sank at Joshua's trumpet call."

It is impossible now to ascertain exactly where
Jericho stood.

Riha, where we found our tents pitched, is supposed to be on the site of 'the city of Palms.' The
village consists of wretched, dirty hovels; the

people being as dirty as their habitations, wild-looking, and very inquisitive. They collected in great numbers close to our encampment.

The next morning, I went out very early to draw. The Arab guard kept off the little children of the village, who were most anxious to approach and examine my camp-stool and drawing-block; and I doubt not they have considered me a witch ever since.

As I sat on an eminence, looking at the land-scape, the question arose—can this be the country we read of? "And Lot lifted up his eyes, and beheld all the plain of Jordan, and it was well watered everywhere before the Lord destroyed Sodom and Gomorrah, even as the garden of Egypt, as thou comest unto Zoar."

Close to our tents was a square tower in ruins. It is undoubtedly of some antiquity, and is asserted to have been the house of Zaccheus; this, however, the traveller may believe, or not, as he pleases. I should have liked to have gone to the Fountain of Elisha, which is said to be connected with the miracle performed there by that prophet; but our stay in Syria was to be but short, and we were obliged to hurry back to Jerusalem: besides, a woman cannot go everywhere and anywhere, and I had not strength to go much out of the beaten path.

I regret I did not find any roses of Jericho (*Anastatica Hierochuntia*), which, although they flower later in the year, are found on the soil, dried and shrivelled up, in the spring months.

Monsieur de Saulcy more than doubts that the *Anastatica Hierochuntia*[1] is the rose of Jericho; and at page 512—513, vol. i., of his ' Journey round the Dead Sea and in Bible Lands,' gives an account of a plant now called (after himself) *Saulcya Hierichuntica*, which I here extract for the benefit of my readers.

" On this plain, which scarcely exhibits a blade of grass, I perceive from my saddle a kind of flower, having some resemblance to a large, dried, Easter daisy, *Pâquerette*; it is quite open, well displayed upon the soil, and looks as if it was alive. On alighting to examine it more closely, I distinguish a plant of the radiated family, but without leaves or petals; in a word, the plant is quite dead; how long it has remained in this state it is impossible to guess. It retains a kind of fantastic existence. I gather a few samples, which I place in my holsters,

[1] In ' Loudon's Encyclopædia of Plants,' this flower is called *Anastatica Hierochuntia*; but in quoting from Monsieur de Saulcy, I have adopted his mode of spelling it.

these having for a long time ceased to be a receptacle for fire-arms, and being daily crammed with stones and plants.

"Another word respecting this extraordinary plant. In the evening when I happened to empty my holsters, I was quite surprised to find the dead flowers closed up, and as dry and hard as if they were made of wood. I then recognized a small flower with a long tap root, which I had never seen alive, but had already picked up at the place where we halted to breakfast on our descent to Ayn-Djedy. What prevented me from ascertaining this identity at first sight was, that one sample was gathered in a state of moisture, whilst the other was picked up perfectly dry. It was then quite clear that this ligneous and exceedingly tough vegetable possessed peculiar properties, which developed themselves hygrometrically, with the corresponding changes of the soil and atmosphere. I immediately tried the experiment, and discovered that the Kaff-Maryam, the rose of Jericho, of the pilgrims, (*Anastatica Hierichuntica*), so celebrated for the same faculty, was not to be compared to my recent discovery. A Kaff-Maryam, placed in water, takes an hour and half before it is entirely open; whilst in the case of my little flower, I watched it visibly expanding, and, without exaggeration, the change was complete in less than three minutes.

" I then recollected the heraldic bearing called the rose of Jericho, which is emblazoned on some escutcheons, dating from the time of the crusades; and I became convinced that I had discovered the real rose of Jericho, long lost sight of after the fall of the Latin kingdom of Jerusalem, and replaced by the anastatica, or Kaff-Maryam, which a Mussulman tradition, accepted by Christians, pointed out to the piety of the early pilgrims, who inquired from the inhabitants of the country what was the plant of the plain of Jericho that never died, and came to life again as soon as it was dipped in water.

" Under any circumstances, this singular hygrometric vegetable constitutes an entirely new genus for botanists, judging by what we know of it, that is to say, by its skeleton. My friend, the Abbé Michon, has undertaken to describe this curious plant, and has paid me the compliment of naming it, *Saulcya Hierichuntica.* Unquestionably the honour is all on my side."

We read of two blind men having been restored to sight by the Saviour, as He left Jericho. We frequently met blind people, during our sojourn in the Holy Land. This calamity seems certainly still to prevail in the east, and to be more common there than in Europe.[1] It was impossible not to think of blind Bartimeus, the son of Timeus, who sat by the wayside, begging; when we met with one, thus afflicted, calling out for alms. Alas! a 'backshish'[2] was the only consolation a traveller had to give him.

We returned from Jericho to Jerusalem by a different road to that we had taken in going, and the ride occupied about seven hours. The scenery

[1] For the common occurrence of blindness in the east, Trench remarks, "There are many causes, the dust and flying sand, pulverized and reduced to minutest particles, enters the eyes, causing inflammations which, being neglected, end frequently in total loss of sight. The sleeping in the open air, on the roofs of the houses, and the consequent exposure of the eyes to the noxious nightly dews, is another source of this malady. A modern traveller calculates that there are four thousand blind in Cairo alone, and another, that you may reckon twenty in every hundred persons. It is true that in Syria the porportion of those afflicted with blindness is not at all so great, yet there also the calamity is of far more frequent occurrence than in western lands; so that we find humane regulations concerning the blind, as concerning a class in the old law." (Lev. xix., 14; Deut. xxvii., 18.

[2] This word is spelt differently by travellers. The right way of spelling it is 'Bak-sheesh,' or 'Bak-shish.' I believe 'Backshish,' as I have written it throughout my journal, to be quite incorrect, though common.

was of the same character as that we had travelled through during the last two days.

We rode round the base of the Mount of Olives, through the Valley of Jehoshaphat, and re-entered the city by St. Stephen's Gate. We had enjoyed the excursion very much, and I could not agree with the person who said he saw nothing at the Dead Sea worth visiting.

The tombs of the kings are to the north of Jerusalem. The portico over the entrance to these tombs is much ornamented with carvings in fruit and flowers. To the left, you enter very small chambers through a low, narrow passage; in each chamber of which there are several empty tombs, and, against the wall, very small niches for lamps.

There are various opinions as to what these excavations were intended for. One attributes them to Helena, Queen of Monobazus, King of Adiabene; others say that they cannot be the tombs of the kings of Judah, as, with the exception of a very few, all the kings were buried in the ' city of David.' These tombs are, however, known by their old name, and probably will ever retain it; although almost every year some fresh traveller starts a new opinion, which he endeavours to persuade the world is the right one.

The cave of Jeremiah is also to the north of the city. It is a very large grotto. One tradition is, that Jeremiah was confined here, and another that he here wrote the Book of Lamentations. Neither tradition is worthy of belief.

While at Jerusalem 1 had an opportunity of visiting a Jewish family in good circumstances, or what is called 'very comfortably off.' On arriving at their house, I was shown into a neat room, furnished with a divan.

The family consisted of a mother (a widow), three sons, and three daughters-in-law, and one little grandson—*only one.* I heard this was a sorrow to the family, for children, especially sons, are considered, as they were in the days of David, a blessing from the Lord. All were Spanish Jews, except the wife of one of the sons, and she was an Italian Jewess.

They were pleased with my visit, and the conversation went on very pleasantly, the lady who accompanied me speaking Spanish fluently, and being a very agreeable interpreter. The mother had been to Carlsbad for her health, had passed through Vienna, seen an opera, travelled on railroads, longed for a railroad at Jerusalem, and ended the account of her journey and all she had seen by saying every thing had "delighted her soul."

Her dress was very pretty.   Over a dark silk petticoat covered by a thin transparent muslin she wore a rich lilac embroidered robe, open in front. It had large hanging sleeves ornamented with handsome coloured braids, and over this robe was a dark lilac silk jacket trimmed with fur, while a diamond ornament fastened to a kerchief of divers colours, was tastefully arranged as a head-dress. Round her neck and wrists she wore many gold chains with diamond clasps.   The three young wives were similarly attired, but their dresses were richer in material, and the ornaments handsomer than those of the mother; their silk robes were embroidered with gold and silver thread, handsome broad girdles were fastened round their waists by golden clasps, and over all were fine cloth jackets with hanging sleeves beautifully embroidered in gold. The head-dress was the Jewish cap or hat, than which nothing can be more ungraceful or unbecoming: it is of silk; stiff, and formal, made on a frame, and bending over the forehead.   Chains of gold and pearls were hung in festoons at the edge of these very ugly head-dresses—from the back of the head fell gauze veils, covered with small flowers in gold work, and numerous handsome jewels adorned the necks and wrists of these ladies.   They were graceful and pleasing, but bashful and retiring, very nearly pretty, with fair complexions and light chestnut coloured hair, but their bad teeth very much diminished their good looks when they smiled.

The only child in the family now made his appearance; he was a pet, as may be well imagined, and a finer, rosier-cheeked little fellow could seldom be seen. From his red cloth cap were suspended many gold coins; and from the back of his neck, hung a tablet, with Hebrew characters on it, which no doubt was a charm—the Jews wearing charms quite as much as the heathens do in this day. The child did not remain long; a most fearful scream which he set up when taken notice of by strangers, obliged his mother to carry him off. This did not disconcert his relatives; they smiled, and seemed to think the tones with which the young heir had welcomed us were harmonious and pleasing.

The gentlemen had the usual long-flowing eastern robe and tarboosh; they were good-looking young men, very fair, and had, like many of the Jews here, auburn hair. While at Jerusalem, I very rarely saw a Jew with the dark complexion or large prominent features, and black hair, which we are accustomed to see in Europe.

The case in which they kept their copy of the law, was shown to us. It was of silver; the exterior, elaborately worked, and of a circular form, standing about a foot and a half high.

Inside this case is the law rolled round silver sticks, which at the end, have small bells also of silver. The reader holds a gilt rod or wand, ornamented with hanging chains, at the end of which rod is a hand made of coral, and he uses this instrument to point with, while he reads out the law.

Coffee, sherbet, and sweetmeats having been offered to us, the family asked us to go and see their private synagogue. It was very small: at the entrance, were shelves, such as one sees in a bookshop, on which were ranged a great many copies of the Old Testament, and commentaries written by various rabbins.

We then took leave of the ladies, as the gentlemen were desirous that we should see one of their public synagogues in the city, to which we accordingly went. Over the entrance-door was an inscription in Hebrew; the exterior was similar to the exterior of those I had seen at Alexandria; the veils or curtains before the shrine, or heykel, in which the law is kept, were of very handsome silk; but everything else looked shabby, and by no means clean.

We went one night on to the roof of the hotel; we were soon wrapped in thought, and, fortunately, in cloaks also—for the air was fresh and crisp. We looked over many flat-roofed houses, the forms of which could scarcely be made out at first; while our eyes wandered in the direction of various spots in the distance, now so familiar to us. The 'sepulchral Valley of Jehoshaphat' was not visible, nor could we see the brook where, as Keble says—

> 'Choose thee out a cell
>   In Kedron's storied dell,
>   Beside the springs of love that never die;
>   Among the olives kneel,
>   The chill night-blast to feel,
>   And watch the moon that saw thy Master's agony.'[1]

But we gazed on the Mount of Olives, which stood clear against the sky, with the moon's light falling upon the most prominent parts of the buildings on the holy hill. A solitary palm, not far from us, stood up, a black spectre, with its huge leaves hanging listlessly by its side; for there was not wind enough to move them up and down, and to cause that indescribable *crackly* sound, the result of the wind waving the heavy boughs to and fro.

It was a half hour in one's life never to be forgotten. Perhaps the shadows which looked so mysterious, added to the almost dead stillness around, made everything more strikingly impressive

[1] 'Christian Year,' Third Sunday in Advent.

at night, than it would have been in the day.   It
was the place and hour to read the Lamentations
of Jeremiah ; but however inclined our minds
might have been to appreciate the scene, our
physique was not so fortunate ; for we began to
feel the increasing cold, and scrambled down a
kind of ladder which led into the hotel, where we
found anything but ' lamentation and woe.'   The
table-d'hôte seemed to be a tower of Babel.   The
gentlemen were in warm and animated conversation, many occupied in planning fresh excursions for
the next day.

CHAPTER X.

JERUSALEM — BETHLEHEM — BETHANY — SCENE IN THE CHURCH
OF THE HOLY SEPULCHRE ON THE EVENING OF GOOD FRIDAY.

THE climate in Syria in April and May is most
agreeable; it is very warm, still not so much so as
to prevent excursions in the middle of the day; we
therefore rode one afternoon to Bethlehem, the city
of the nativity.   As we left Jerusalem, the valley of
Rephaim [1] was on the right of the road to Bethlehem.

The well of the Magi, which has been fixed upon as
the place where the three wise men of the East first
saw the star, is between Jerusalem and Bethlehem.
We passed also the Greek convent of Elijah, it
is picturesque, and near a grove of olive trees.   A
field to the left was pointed out as the one where

[1] 2 Samuel v. 18, 22.

the angel appeared to the shepherds, bringing them " good tidings of great joy, which should be to all people," and where " a multitude of the heavenly host were heard praising God, and saying, Glory to God in the highest, and on earth peace, good will towards men." [1]   Nor could we look on the fields without remembering the story of Ruth, the scene of which was at Bethlehem.

Bethlehem was called Bethlehem Judah, to distinguish it from Bethlehem in Zebulon; it is beautifully situated, standing on a height, and there is an appearance of comfort and civilization as one approaches the olive groves, fig trees, and gardens planted close to the town, such as one does not see either outside or inside the walls of Jerusalem.

On reaching Bethlehem, a little Syrian child greeted me with " How do you do ?"

I scarcely had expected that the first word I should hear in the city of the nativity would be English.

At the end of the town are Greek, Latin and Armenian churches.

We went first to the church of St. Mary of Bethlehem, or the Church of the Nativity, originally built by Helena, the mother of Constantine.

As we entered, boys pursued us, offering rosaries,

---

[1] St. Luke ii. 13, 14.

and carvings in mother of pearl for sale; and old Thomas (the guide) could scarcely keep these troublesome people from annoying us every minute.

Under the chancel is the Cave of the Nativity. We descended to it by a flight of steps. In a recess a few feet above the ground, there is a stone slab, on it the representation of a star. This marks the spot where it is said the Saviour was born. From the ceiling of the recess hung several lighted lamps. A similar place is shewn where the manger was.

Near the cave is the Chapel of the Innocents, where, strange to say, the good people of Bethlehem believe they are buried under the altar! and in this chapel is also shewn the tomb or St. Jerome.

A service was going on in the Armenian church; at the altar, young boys were chanting, and many women sitting on the ground staring about them. Not far from the village is the Grotto of the Virgin, where she and the holy child were concealed before they fled into Egypt.

As we returned to Jerusalem, we met a great number of persons on the road—all addressed us with a kind word or two—the Greeks with a gentle ' bona sera '—a Bedouin, on a camel, with a solemn, gruff ' mashallah!'

The path we were traversing being the nearest

from Bethlehem to Jerusalem is, we may reason-
ably think, that over which our Saviour was carried "when they brought Him to Jerusalem to
present Him to the Lord." This afternoon's ride
was, therefore, one of intense interest. Old Thomas
jogged on before on his pony, every now and then
saying, "Lady, take me to England.' It was in
vain I told him he would not be happy there, and
that he had better stay in his own country. He
was a very crusty old man; but his conversation
always amused me, especially his quaint and blunt
remarks. One evening, while I was sketching,
some Arab woman, completely concealed in drapery,
came up to me; Thomas said, "Great shame Arab
woman shut up her face." On one occasion, I told
him to go and see if the Church of the Holy Sepulchre were open, as I wished to go there. "Well,
I go," said Thomas; "and, if it shut, you say,
Thomas, all your fault." I felt half inclined to
say, "Thomas, you are a *very* cross old man."

Next to Bethlehem, the village of Bethany is
most eagerly visited by Christians of all denominations, when they come to the Holy Land.

Going there we skirted the foot of the Mount of
Olives.

Occasionally, we caught glimpses of the Dead

Sea. Olives, almonds, and fig-trees grew on the sides of hills, and in the ravines; and, though by no means in great numbers, were still numerous enough to break the monotony of the rocky ground and stony valleys.

Bethany is beautifully situated, and is one of the prettiest spots in the neighbourhood of Jerusalem —so retired and peaceful. Of course the site of Mary's house, and the abode of Simon the leper, are shown.

We descended several steps into the tomb of Lazarus, holding lighted tapers. Whatever difference of opinion there may be to its being the real tomb or not, all agree as to the village being Bethany. And who could say whether we did not gaze on the very spot where Jesus's greatest miracle was performed,[1] and stand near

'The blessed home, where Jesus deign'd to stay,
    The peaceful home to zeal sincere
        And contemplation dear,
    Where Martha lov'd to wait, with reverence meet,
    And wiser Mary lingered at His sacred feet.'[2]

On our return from Bethany we saw what is thought to be the site of Bethpage.

[1] There is a tradition that the first question Lazarus asked our Lord after his resurrection, was, if he should have to die again, and on hearing that he must of necessity do so, that he never smiled afterwards.

[2] Keble's 'Christian Year,' Advent Sunday.

During our stay at Jerusalem, I went one morning, at six o'clock, to attend the early service, which was performed in Hebrew, for the converted Jews. The congregation was very small. The interior of the church is simple, and in good taste. The clerk, a baptized Jew, told me that his family and himself had been converted to Christianity a few years ago.

On the Sunday preceding Holy week, the baptism of a Jew took place in the church. I was present; it was a very interesting sight. The godfather and godmother of the man were English residents at Jerusalem.

I did not forget to see the spurs, sword, and heavy chain and cross, which belonged to Godfrey de Bouillon, the first Latin king of Jerusalem, who, it is said, refused to wear a diadem in the city where his Saviour had worn a crown of thorns.

Just before we quitted Jerusalem, a gentleman had left it for Damascus, and had proceeded some miles on his journey, when he recollected he had not seen the above-mentioned spurs and sword. He instantly turned his horse's head, rode back to Jerusalem hastened into the vestry of the Latin chapel in the Church of the Holy Sepulchre, where the relics are kept, and after examining them carefully, resumed his journey. I hope he did not meet some matter-of-fact individual, who told him he was quite mistaken, and that he had not seen the veritable spurs and sword of Godfrey de Bouillon.

Preparations were going on at the beginning of Passion week in the Church of the Holy Sepulchre for the various ceremonies which take place at that season. I went to the church early one morning, and found that in the space between the entrance to the Holy Sepulchre and the gates of the large Greek church, arrangements were being made by priests of the Roman Catholic faith for a mass.

An altar stood close to the door leading into the sepulchre. This altar was faced with silver, and had flowers and large candlesticks on it. I was astonished at seeing them lighted by priests of different churches. On enquiry, I found some of these large tapers belonged to the Latin, others were the property of the Greek and Armenian churches.

Benches and chairs were put for the congregation. I saw the pilgrims I had met on board the boat from Alexandria to Jaffa arrive, many French Sisters of Charity, in their simple dress, and at last the French Consul came in a very gay

uniform. He was preceded by several Janissa-
ries, who marched with large sticks mounted in
silver, which they struck forcibly on the pavement
as they came along, making the pilgrims, Sisters of
Charity, and me, almost start from our seats.
There was an excellent seraphine, played in a
masterly manner by a monk. Four or five more
sang beautifully, generally in quartetts, their voices
were so rich and powerful they filled every corner
of the large church; but I must own *all was more
theatrical than devotional.* The music, though
beautiful, did not suit the sacredness of the
words.

After this mass was over, I went into the Holy
Sepulchre. A priest was lighting the numerous
lamps which hung over the sepulchre, as also
several candles on the altar; the candlesticks
were gilt figures of angels holding the tapers.
There was a small silver gilt cabinet, with doors
very richly worked, on it three gilt figures, representing our Saviour, and two saints. `I stayed some
little time. While I was there, a priest came in
with a large packet of rosaries and crosses. They
were placed on the altar, he recited a short prayer,
then blessed the things he had brought, which
probably were distributed afterwards to the Roman

Catholic visitors, who had come to Jerusalem for Easter.

Although I had heard that we should be anything but gratified at seeing the ceremonies that take place on the evening of Good Friday in the Church of the Holy Sepulchre, we felt reluctant to be absent on the occasion. Everybody was talking of going, and, as everybody went, we also proceeded thither about seven o'clock in the evening. I had not been long there, when I most devoutly wished I had not gone.

In different parts of the church, priests were preaching in various languages to surrounding pilgrims. There were processions preceded and followed by crowds of people. Little boys dressed in white surplices, carrying lighted tapers, and singing painfully out of tune. Then there was a sudden rush up the staircase to the Chapel of the Crucifixion,[1] where a scene took place which can never be effaced from my memory. An image, the size of life, intended to represent our Saviour on

[1] It is well known that the chapels of the crucifixion and exaltation of the cross are supposed to be on Mount Calvary, and the rotunda where the Holy Sepulchre stands to be on the site of the garden of Joseph of Arimathea. The site of Mount Calvary is, however, a point in dispute among the learned of the present day.

the cross, was laid on the ground, and a German pilgrim preached in very energetic language on the sufferings and death of our Lord.

In several other parts of the church, the same subject was dilated on in different languages. The image was taken down, afterwards, to the stone of unction, and anointed. What must the Mahomedans have thought of all the ceremonies enacted on that evening? Was there not enough to make them believe that all Eastern Christian churches at Jerusalem had, at least on one occasion, set up idols in the house of God?

The pressure of the crowd was very great; the constant chattering and remarks of all around must have disturbed any inclined to pious and serious thoughts; but there was no devotional feeling apparent anywhere, except on the part of the preachers; all present were staring, whispering, wondering. Short people on tip-toes, trying to look over tall people's shoulders — young children, half stifled in the confusion and heat, endeavouring to find a passage through a mass of human beings—while the Turkish soldiers tried in vain to keep the Christians in order.

We had seen enough, and by dint of much elbowing, and treading on our neighbours' feet, we extricated ourselves from the crowd, and regained the hotel. I heard afterwards that the image was finally placed in the sepulchre.

On the following morning we were to leave Jerusalem for Damascus, but before our departure, I returned to the Holy Sepulchre, wishing that the last impression of it should be agreeable to me. All was quiet. An early Latin mass was going on, attended by but very few persons. An altar placed near the entrance of the sepulchre prevented my entering it, which I regretted very much.

I stayed some little time looking at everything in the church, feeling I should never return there, and reluctant to quit a place of which I thought I could never see enough.

CHAPTER XI.

IT was necessary that we should arrive at Beyrout by a certain day, in order to meet the steamer which goes from thence to Alexandria; it was, therefore, impossible to remain for Easter Sunday at Jerusalem. This I regretted very much for some reasons, though by no means anxious again to witness scenes similar to those which had taken place on the evening of Good Friday.

Our journey being arranged, we started for

Damascus in high spirits, though the weather did not smile on us, and many a well-meaning person said, " I fear it will rain;" others shook their heads when the journey was mentioned, while some said we should not go far before we returned to Jerusalem.

We left the city by the Damascus Gate. I never regretted leaving any place so much as I regretted leaving Jerusalem; and, as we lingered to take a farewell view of it, I thought how much 1 had left there unexplored. Owing to indisposition, and the rainy weather, I had lost some days of 'sight-seeing.' It is not difficult to re-visit spots in Europe which have pleased one; but the Holy Land is not often visited twice in one's life. I therefore left 'the city of David' with the sad reflection, I should never see it again. It was about half a mile from Jerusalem that we had the last glimpse of the Mount of Olives. The day was dull and cloudy, which, probably, made the surrounding scenery appear more than usually forlorn and wasted. We had scarcely been an hour on the road when the sky became threatening, and we could see showers falling on the distant hills.

A bad cold, which I had caught a few days before, suddenly increased in a most provoking manner, and my voice was nearly gone. I thought of our weather-wise friends, and of what they would say. " Wasn't I right?—did I not tell them they shouldn't go?" Every step we took things became worse, and at last we could deceive ourselves no longer. Rain fell in good earnest. I rode quickly after the litter, in order to take shelter in it; but, when we reached it, one of the mules was kicking furiously. It was better not to stop; and I rode on.

We arrived at Bethel just as our tents were pitched, and hurried into them, although they were as yet unfurnished.

At dinner time we looked at each other with grave faces, but said nothing. The tents were not like those in India, calculated to keep out such rain as it seemed likely we should have. The ground outside had become quite saturated. The wind blew and unfastened the tent pegs; the rain came in, and we sat in cloaks and India rubber shoes trying to look cheerfully on the present and future. We soon retired to our beds. It was bitter cold, the wind increased, the rain fell in torrents, and in the middle of the night poured in on the foot of my bed. My meditations, for I could not sleep, were not agreeable; I thought of cholera, fevers, all kinds of disasters. It was really a sad prospect we had before us. To remain at Bethel the next day in the rain would be anything but pleasant; to return to Jerusalem, and give up the journey to Damascus, very provoking and disappointing; to go on to Nabulus (our next encamping place) in the rain, very imprudent. In any case we were certain of being wet through; I, therefore, made up my mind that it would be as well to go on to Nabulus and trust to its being fine on the morrow. When I got up in the morning, at Bethel, everything was concealed by the mist, and it was vain to think of going out before breakfast. The time was fully occupied in reading all about this place, or "house of God," which is the signification of the word Bethel—its original name was Luz—and here it was that Jacob commemorated his vision by raising a pillar, and calling the place Bethel, instead of Luz. It will be remembered, also, that it was the southern seat of the worship of the golden calf.[1] It is frequently mentioned in the Old Testament, being often alluded to in Amos. "For, saith the Lord God unto the house of Israel, seek ye me, and ye shall live; but seek not Bethel, nor enter into

---

[1] 1 Kings xii. 29—33; xiii. 1.

Gilgal, and pass not to Beersheba; for Gilgal shall surely go into captivity, and Bethel shall come to nought." [1]

The weather prevented our seeing the ruins that still exist of Bethel. I merely saw a dilapidated tower on a hill, and I looked in vain for oaks through the mist, for no one could forget that touching story of Deborah, Rachael's nurse, being buried under an oak near Bethel, which was thenceforth called the " Oak of Weeping."

Occasionally our prospects looked better. The sun struggled hard to disperse the angry black clouds, but the latter would not give way, and shower after shower fell, till the ground was a complete swamp. I was carried in a chair to the tent in which breakfast was served, and carried back! Then we held a consultation whether to go on to Nabulus, or return to Jerusalem. This important question was carried by a majority of two against one. It certainly was a doleful day; sometimes the sun peeped out, and then hurried in again, leaving us to despair, and to repeated torrents of rain. Preparations for starting began, the tents were struck (except mine, which was kept up to the last moment, and in which we were all

[1] Amos v. 5.

huddled.) No one spoke—no one could give any comfort to his neighbour. Detached sentences were sometimes heard. " We never thought of rain," said one. *" It is a very unusual season,"* remarked another ; and so it was, for at this time of year in Syria it is always fine, though not too hot. When at last all was ready, we began our march, the guide leading the way. The horse he rode was laden with large paniers, camp-stools, and even a small table. The way he mounted the animal was very droll: he first climbed up behind, reaching the saddle on his stomach, he then turned himself over on his back, and, rising on his knees, settled himself in a manner that appeared to be most uncomfortable, by placing one leg on the top of the table, and the other on the camp-stools. It was a cold morning, and the rain beat into the litter in which I was unfortunately travelling. It is almost impossible to see much in this most uncomfortable conveyance. Although we could not see Shiloh, we knew it to be between Bethel and Shechem. Its situation is mentioned in the Bible as on the " north side of Bethel, on the east side of the highway that goeth up from Bethel to Shechem, and on the south of Lebonah." [1]

[1] Judges xxi, 19.

Modern travellers identify Lebonah with Lebban, a place surrounded by hills.

At Shiloh the ark remained from the days of Joshua till it was carried with the army that marched againt the Philistines.   We read in Jeremiah, that when God exhorts the Jews to " amend their ways, and their doings," [1] they are threatened, unless they repent, with the same judgment as Shiloh.   " But go ye now unto my place which was in Shiloh, where I set my name at the first, and see what I did to it for the wickedness of my people Israel.   Therefore will I do unto this house, which is called by my name, wherein ye trust, and unto the place which I gave to you and your fathers, as I have done to Shiloh." [2]

The day cleared up towards noon, and I could see we were passing through a very pleasant country. There were valleys and ravines, where grew large olive-trees and many orchards of figs.   The orchards were separated from each other by low stone walls. Occasionally we passed a village looking anything but prosperous.

The scenery as we approached Nabulus, the ancient Shechem, was very pretty.   The valleys were cultivated, the hills wooded with groves of

[1] Jeremiah vii. 3.   [2] *Ibid.*, vii. 12, 14.

large olive-trees, standing in beds of lovely wild-flowers—among them the delicate cyclamen, and a large white arum just peeping out of the ground. Droves of donkeys laden with sacks, a boy driving them, and a little bird with white and black plumage, were the only animated creatures to be seen during the day's journey.

When I reached a grove of trees about a mile from Nabulus, and crept out of my litter, F—— was not to be found, and no one had seen him for some time. This was anything but pleasant intelligence; but I was somewhat relieved by hearing he had with him one of the Turkish soldiers, who had come from Jerusalem as our escort. At last he appeared, having ridden on to the consul's house to ascertain whether we could find shelter in the town. Though the rain had ceased, it threatened to be very damp and cold, if one remained in tents for the night; but not finding accommodation, we waited for the luggage. The evening was drawing in—it was chilly, and the ground wet—the sun was setting with a very sulky countenance, as if he had no intention of rising the next morning in a better humour: every now and then he looked through a dense grey cloud, then disappeared, sending down a few rays illuminating the misty summit of a hill, the sides of which were fringed with olive-trees.

When the baggage arrived we heard we were not at the right encamping ground, and that we must go beyond the town of Nabulus; but, alas ! when I got into the litter, it was found that the harness of one of the mules was broken, and I was borne by the Arabs. At last we reached the spot where the tents were to be pitched; it was quite dark. It seemed as if the whole town of Na-bulus had come out to see us, the crowd was so great; and there were more useless than useful people about us. At last lanterns were obtained, unpacking began, every one ran in the wrong direction, everybody scolding each other, the thing most wanted was not to be found, and what was not necessary abounded on all sides. In the midst of the confusion a horse got loose, and rushed in among men and boxes ; but it was caught before it could do much mischief. In the meantime, my maid and I sat squeezed up together in the litter till the tents were ready. It was too cold to sit up, so we retired to rest.

The next morning was fine, and it seemed as if we should now go on prosperously.

The spot on which we had encamped was very

lovely. We were entirely surrounded by olive-trees. The ancient town of Shechem, now called Nabulus, is situated in a lovely valley enclosed by Mounts Ebal and Gerizem, and is very picturesque.

Shechem is mentioned so early as Abraham's time.[1] In the history of Jacob it is frequently alluded to, and is repeatedly read of in other places in the Old Testament. It subsequently received the name of Neapolis from the Romans.

"On Mount Ebal Joshua built an altar unto the Lord God of Israel." On Ebal were assembled half the tribes—on Gerizem the other half—to hear the maledictions pronounced on all who should break the law of God, and to listen to the blessings bestowed on those who should obey it.

Jeroboam, king of Israel, built Shechem, and made it the capital of his dominions, and it still existed during the exile of the Jews. Both the city and temple, which stood on Mount Gerizem, were destroyed 129 B.C. by John Hyrcanus.

The most interesting object near Nabulus is Jacob's well, where our Saviour sat weary and thirsty, and where the woman of Samaria came to draw water, His conversation with whom caused many of that city to believe on Him. The depth of the well is ascertained to be seventy-five feet.

[1] Genesis xii. 6.

We had but little time to tarry at Nabulus, so we mounted our horses, riding in the direction of Djenin.

We soon passed the present town of Samaria, which is on a high hill to the left of our road.

The scenery in the vicinity is beautiful. Our road lay through grassy ravines, watered by clear brooks, shaded by olive-trees. At one of the brooks were women washing clothes. They had many gold and silver coins strung together, and fastened on each side of the head—a style of head-dress I had not seen among the peasantry here.

Samaria, which means "watch height," was built by Omri, king of Israel, about 925 B.C. It will be remembered that it was here " Ahab reared up an altar for Baal in the house of Baal, which he had built in Samaria."

The city, like Shechem, was destroyed by John Hyrcanus, but was subsequently rebuilt with great magnificence by Herod the Tetrarch.

There are some very interesting ruins to be seen, among them a church where it is said John the Baptist was buried.

We were delighted with the appearance of the country; the valleys were richly cultivated, and, when we gained any considerable elevation, the landscape was equally pleasing; in the distance we could see fertile and well-watered plains, and where the land was not cultivated it was carpeted with wild flowers, which covered also every spot of ground we passed over, growing close up to the dark trunks of the olive trees.

The bright and cheerful aspect of the country made one almost think the land had not been "laid most desolate because of all the abominations which they had committed;"[1] it seemed rather as if showers of blessings had commenced, and that "the tree of the field was yielding her fruit, and the earth her increase."[2]

After descending a rocky hill we entered a lovely valley, where we dismounted and rested for an hour.

While there, three Arabs armed with guns came up to us; they merely stopped, stared at us, and went on their way.

Before we reached Djenin we saw several villages on wooded heights; at a distance they looked imposing, but the houses are no doubt, like those of all the villages of this country, in a very ruinous state. In a narrow valley, before we reached Djenin, a fox ran on before us and climbing a steep

[1] Ezekiel xxxiii. 29.   [2] Ezekiel xxxiv. 27.

bank, stopped, gazed at us for a minute, and disappeared.

When we got to Djenin we missed one of our party, and in about ten minutes after our arrival he rode up to the tents. We soon heard he had met with an adventure. It appears that riding a little way behind he had missed us at a sharp turn, and taken a wrong road; two Arabs met him thus alone, stopped him, pointed their guns at him, and one attempted to seize his horse's bridle, when our friend riding at the man, knocked him down, and galloped off at full speed, the men throwing stones after him. It is probable their guns were not loaded; had they been so he might not have come off so easily.

Djenin, which signifies 'the fountain of the garden,' is believed to be the En-gannim of holy Scripture, and is mentioned in the fifteenth chapter of Joshua, thirty-fourth verse, as one of the inheritances of the tribe of Judah.

Our tents were pitched on a rising ground near the town, which is very prettily situated in a grove of trees; overtopping all were a few date-palms: to the north was the valley of Esdraelon, which we were to traverse the next day, and the hills of Nazareth backed by Jebel ed Dahi, or the little Hermon.

We had taken the litter with us in case of accident, and in the event of any of the party being unable to ride. I should recommend all ladies who undertake a journey through Syria to have a litter, it is certainly a prudent step.

I found my maid very unwell the morning after we arrived at Djenin, and had it not been for the litter we should have been detained a day at that place.

After leaving Djenin the next morning, we entered on the plain of Esdraelon; the hills of Gilboa, which are memorable for the battle between Saul and the Philistines, when the sons of the former were killed, and where he himself fell by his own hand, were plainly visible. We were all day in a beautiful and fertile country, passing over a narrow path strewn with flowers; among which was a pink convolvolus, which crept humbly along the ground, disappearing among the fields of grain. Every flower reminded me of the saying of our Lord: "Consider the lilies of the field how they grow, they toil not neither do they spin; and yet I say unto you, that even Solomon in all his glory was not arrayed like one of these;"[1] and every field I passsed brought before me the parable of the tares[2] and the sower.

---

[1] Matthew vi. 28, 29.

[2] 'The field is the world,' words few and slight as they

The valley we were in is called, in sacred history, the valley of Jezreel, and the valley of Megiddo, and here was fought the great battle when Josiah, king of Judah, was killed. In the first chapter of the book of Judith, eighth verse, the valley is called " the great plain of Esdraelon."

Mount Tabor was to our right, and we were in the neighbourhood of places familiar to us in the Old and New Testament. Jezreel, not very distant, recalled the sad story of Ahab and Jezebel; —Nain, the raising to life of the widow's son by Jesus; Cana, our Lord's first miracle; and Endor, where dwelt the woman with the 'familiar spirit,' to whom Saul went, and where Samuel appeared to him, and told him he and his sons should be WITH HIM (Samuel) on the morrow, and the host of Israel should be delivered into the hand of the Philistines.

Mount Tabor rises very suddenly from the plain, and stands quite unconnected with any smaller hill. It was clothed with herbage, but, as it seemed, somewhat sparingly with trees and bushes.

This mountain has always been regarded as that

may seem, a great battle has been fought over them, greater, perhaps, than over any single phrase in the Scripture, if we except the consecrating words at the Holy Eucharist. *Notes on the Parables*, by *R. C. Trench.*

where the scene of the transfiguration took place.[1]
Could there be another ride fraught with more
interesting associations than that of this day on
the plain of Esdraelon?

It was a perfect spring day, the air was balmy,
and the birds were singing. After resting an hour
on the grass in the middle of the day, we remounted
our horses, and rode on to Nazareth. When we
reached the hills of Galilee, we missed the guide
and an English servant: on ascending the hill and
looking down into the valley of Esdraelon, we
could see no appearance of them. In the meantime the litter, which had preceded us, went on,
wound round the hill, and disappeared also. F——
and I began to toil up the steep side of the hill, in
hopes of overtaking the litter, but on reaching the
top no litter was in sight. One gentleman of our
party rode back in order to ascertain why the
guide and servant had remained behind.

The road became almost impassable: our horses
climbed over high rocks, and slid down stony slabs,
till at last the way was completely blocked up by a
precipitous ledge of rock, over which poured a cata-

[1] In Psalm lxxxix., where the majesty and power of God
are alluded to, the psalmist exclaims—" Tabor and Hermon
shall rejoice in Thy name."

ract of water. After scrambling about for some
time among great heaps of stone, we returned to
the place where our friend had left us to go in
search of the missing servants; we saw horsemen
coming along the plain, but only *two*—the Arab
guide was not there.   Although I had scarcely
recovered the fright caused by missing two of our
party, and by riding over the very bad road we had
just left, I could not help being extremely amused
at the ridiculous appearance of the man-servant.
He was seated on the guide's horse, on either side
of which were a large hamper and several camp-
stools.   There the wretched man sat crumpled up,
looking much ashamed of himself—his knees touching his face, and scarcely able to maintain his
balance.   The cause of his absence had been his
horse having broke loose, and the guide having
gone in pursuit of it, since which neither guide nor
horse had re-appeared.   After a considerable lapse
of time, the Englishman mounted the heavy-laden
steed of the guide, and followed us.   Being under
no apprehension for the safety of the Arab, we
began to think of our own, and were lucky enough
to find the road to Nazareth.   Evening was approaching, and it would not have been wise to pass the
night amongst these wild hills without any guard;

for the Bedouins, who are met with sometimes in the day, might not be civil to strangers in the dark. It was, indeed, more from "good luck than good management" that we found ourselves on the right road.

Descending the hills, we entered a narrow valley, with flowery banks on each side; and at last, after a very fatiguing journey, reached the tents which were pitched opposite the town of Nazareth, and close to the well of Miriam.

To complete this chapter of accidents, we heard on our arrival that the litter had been upset in a rocky path, and my maid, who was in it, pulled out by the muleteer; fortunately, however, she was very little hurt.

CHAPTER XII.

NAZARETH—MOUNT OF PRECIPITATION—WELL OF MIRIAM—WOMEN
OF NAZARETH—FRANCISCAN CHURCH AND CONVENT—GREEK
CHURCH — RIDE TO TIBERIAS — BEAUTIFUL WILD FLOWERS—
SCENERY—TIBERIAS—SITES OF CAPERNAUM—MAGDALA—BETH-
SAIDA AND CHORAZIN—RIDE TO SAFED—RUIN OF OLD CASTLE
AT SAFED—JEBEL-ESH-SHEIKH—RIDE TO BANIAS—CASTLE OF
BANIAS—SOURCE OF THE JORDAN—JOURNEY TO DAMASCUS.

NAZARETH stands on a hill. It is like all the towns
and villages in Syria—the streets are dirty, and
the habitations in bad repair. What is called 'the
Mount of Precipitation,'[1] is three miles from the
present town.

The monks of the Latin convent at Nazareth,
however, maintain that it is rightly named, and
that the city in the time of our Lord extended that
far.

Miriam's, or Mary's Well, was very near our

[1] St. Luke, iv .29.

tents. It was surrounded late in the evening and early in the morning by women, many of whom were beautiful, with graceful figures; they came to 'fill their water-pots with water,' and formed themselves into the most picturesque groups, some standing with vases on their heads, some sitting, others leaning on the edge of the well—all talking, laughing, and no doubt gossiping of the latest news of Nazareth and its neighbourhood, for a well in the East, to which women resort to draw water, is known to be a kind of *female club.*

The manners of the women of Nazareth were not as agreeable as their appearance. They crowded round me when I went into the town, some taking hold of my gown and shawl to examine them, while laughing girls,—and lovely, merry little children ran on before me to look under my bonnet. It was at first amusing; but they became so troublesome, I was glad to get back to my tent.

The Franciscan church and convent are in the town, and the Roman Catholics assert that the real grotto of the Annunciation is in their church—but the Greeks maintain that their church stands on the site of the house where the Virgin dwelt when the angel was sent and addressed her with those words,

"Hail! thou that art highly favoured—the Lord is with thee—blessed art thou among women."

On the door leading into the Greek church are crosses, chalices, and bottles, carved in stone. I remarked that the form of the bottles is much like that of those still used by the peasantry of the neighbourhood.

The interior, as is the case with all the Greek churches in Syria, is very much ornamented. The screen, which separates the body of the church from the chancel, is, I was told, of cedar wood; it is very richly carved, with two doors opening into the chancel. On the top of the screen are carved heads of angels and doves, and large crosses, and several compartments or panels, in which are paintings, portraying the life of our blessed Saviour and the Virgin. The carvings of the pulpit are painted of different colours, and in bad taste. The church is full of indifferent, but very ancient and in-teresting pictures, the subject of several being the annunciation of the Virgin. There is one evidently much prized, as before it hangs a curtain; it is not, however, a painting, but worked in very small, coloured beads—the subject, the angel Gabriel's visit to Mary. Her dress is of small white glittering pearls, exceedingly pretty, while that of the angel is worked with gold beads.

In a small chapel, under the altar, is a well, the water of which is excellent. The walls of the chapel were in panels, in which were pretty patterns, some of coloured tiles, others of marble.

When we left the church, an old man, with a long, white beard, was seated on a step at the door, reading the Bible. He removed his spectacles for a moment, looked at us, and resumed his studies; and although I remained to take a sketch of him, he did not take any notice of us, but continued

> 'Unfolding
> His immortal book,
> In that silent mirror, for himself to look.
>
> *
>
> In this quiet haven,
>   Pondering o'er his soul,
> And how much is graven
>   On the solemn scroll
> Which, to worlds assembled, judgment shall unroll.'

All the places here connected with the history of our Saviour are shown by the guides. A stone, where our Lord is said to have dined, is pointed out; also Joseph's shop. We should be satisfied with knowing that it was at Nazareth our Lord lived, before he entered on His ministry, and that He there passed His childhood, and much of His early life.[1]

[1] St. Luke ii. 39—51.

During the night it rained very much, and I feared we should encounter new troubles, asking myself when I rose in the morning, " What will be our adventures to day on our road to the Sea of Tiberias ?"

After leaving Nazareth, we ascended a very steep hill, from whence we had a fine view of the Valley of Esdraelon and Mount Tabor ; we then entered on a plain extending nearly as far as Tiberias, our horses threading their way through fertile fields, over a path covered with anemones, blue lupines, and a profusion of the most beautiful wild flowers, that grew in such luxuriance as to be on a level with their heads, and which rendered our route plainly distinguishable for several miles in advance.

Half-way between Nazareth and Tiberias, we met several European travellers of our acquaintance, returning from the latter place. All had something to complain of more or less. A German count urged us to have a guard at the Sea of Tiberias— what had happened to the poor man there we had not time to hear. Then a French gentleman passed us quickly, saying something about " la grande chaleur," with which, I am sorry to say, he associated the name of " le diable," while a French lady had a woeful tale about scorpions and snakes !

In spite of these sad accounts, we went on, and soon came in sight of the lake.

The top of Mount Hermon far, far away, was covered with snow; on the other side of the lake were hills, the base of which apparently touched the water, in which the blue sky, hills, and white fleecy clouds were all alike reflected. Presently we came upon the town, which seems, to rest almost on the bosom of the lake, long grass and wild flowers growing close up to the ruined towers and walls.

The greater part of the place was destroyed not many years ago by an earthquake. It has a very desolate look. To the right of the town are extremely high rocky hills, which slope down to the lake,—further off, are the baths of Tiberias, and still higher hills, and in the extreme distance, the snowy mountain I have spoken of. It is a fine, grand view.

When close to the town, I heard a shout, and perceived that the litter was completely overturned. In a minute more, I saw the muleteer dive into it, and bring out my little maid, lifting her high up in the air, and setting her all right on her feet! She was not hurt; but I sincerely hoped that this would be the end of *her* misadventures.

She was so brave—so good humoured—that although it was impossible not to laugh, I was extremely vexed at this second mischance of the litter.

The tents were on the shore of the lake, and to the left was the town. Towards dusk the wind arose and "the sea" became much agitated.

How much there was to think of as we sat on the shore, beholding the very waters on which our Saviour walked to His disciples, bidding them "not to be afraid," and where He calmed the tempest with His gentle words, "peace! be still!"

It was to the east of the lake that Jesus fed the five thousand—

> " Here may we sit and dream
> Over the heavenly theme,
> Till to our soul the former days return—
> Till on the grassy bed, where thousands once He fed,
> The world's incarnate maker we discern."

The sea of Galilee does not exceed eleven or twelve miles in length, and five or six in breadth.[1] The river Jordan falls into it at the north, and runs out of it at the south.

Tiberias was built by the Tetrarch, Herod Antipas, and called after the Emperor Tiberius.

---

[1] It is first mentioned in Numbers xxxiv. 11, where it is called the Sea of Chinnereth. In the Gospels it is the Sea of Gennesaret, as well as that of Galilee and Tiberias.

The hot baths are at a short distance from the town. We had not time to visit them, as we were obliged to reach Safed by sunset, and it was a long day's journey.

Leaving Tiberias, and the valley in which it stands, we ascended a hill, " the sea " being on our right. The road wound for some time along a high rocky bank overhanging the water ; the flowers were more abundant, if possible, than they had as yet been during our journey, and mingled with low shrubs and long grass, that extended down to the very edge of the water—

> " Where Gennesaret's wave
> Delights the flowers to lave
> That o'er the Western Slope, breathe airs of balm."

We were near the site of Capernaum, where our Lord resided often, after His ministry had begun, and against which He pronounced this heavy denunciation, " And thou, Capernaum, which art exalted unto Heaven, shalt be brought down to Hell, for if the mighty works which have been done in thee had been done in Sodom, it would have remained unto this day. But I say unto you, that it shall be more tolerable for the land of Sodom in the day of judgment than for thee." [1]

[1] Matthew xi. 23—24.

Here also, on the western shore, was Magdala, supposed to be the birth-place of Mary Magdalene.

Bethsaida and Chorazin, to the inhabitants of which the Saviour likewise addressed the same awful words as He did to Capernaum, were not far from us. Josephus, in mentioning this country, among other remarks, says, " The country named Gennesar extends along the lake, wonderful both for its nature and beauty." It was certainly a lovely ride. When we quitted the lake, the road led up a steep, rocky hill ; but, wherever we turned, we still saw the lake of Tiberias.

There was a constant change of scenery. At one time we ascended stony heights, then descended into beautiful ravines, well wooded and watered, with oleanders growing nearly in the brooks.

The morning had been hitherto all that could be wished—fresh, sunny, with large clouds causing a continual change of light and shade on the landscape, but towards noon the day became overcast— and when, on reaching a ravine, where we found water, trees, and deep shade—and which was a place perfectly well suited for our midday rest, we dismounted and arranged our repast, ominous-looking clouds warned us we should soon be disturbed, and that a storm was impending. We had, in fact, just begun an attack on a cold fowl, when the rain fell in torrents, and we rushed in all directions to seek shelter where we could best find it, as the olive-tree, under which we had bivouacked was not sufficient protection from such a deluge. After this disaster, we thought it advisable to hasten on to Safed. The scenery was still very lovely as we ascended the hills; and, at every turn of the way, we still looked down on Lake Tiberias. Approaching Safed, the country became more wooded, the fields cultivated, and the green valleys and ravines studded with trees and flowers of every colour.

The town of Safed,[1] which is on a considerable height, was now visible, looking very picturesque and imposing. We rode through a portion of it to reach our tents, which were on an open space of ground in a beautiful situation. Here again the Sea of Tiberias was visible; to our left we had some part of the town as a foreground, while to the right were the ruins of a castle, high above that part of the hill on which Safed stands.

An earthquake destroyed a great part of Safed

---

[1] Safed being the only town in the neighbourhood on an eminence, it is supposed to be the one alluded to by our Lord, when, in His Sermon, he says, " A city that is set on a hill cannot be hid."—Matthew v. 14.

in 1837; and, though many buildings have been restored, the town still contains not a few ruinous houses and walls.   The place is considered peculiarly sacred by the Jews, as they affirm our Lord will reign near the lake of Tiberias for forty years previous to His going to Jerusalem.

The women of Safed wear the nose-ring.   I had not seen this custom before in Syria; and in this case it was not a pendant ring, but a small, round button, fitting close to the nose.

The prospect from the old castle is very fine and extensive.   We could see the landscape extending even beyond the Jordan.

The next morning, a very ridiculous occurrence took place.   A misunderstanding arose between the guide and a Janissary, who had accompanied us from Jerusalem.   The former, a man of gigantic strength, seized the latter by the collar, shaking him as a terrier does a rat.   The poor Janissary could not disengage himself from the grasp of his adversary, and it seemed likely he would have been shaken into bits, had not an English servant rushed forward, calling out 'Row, row,' meaning to say 'Rooh, rooh,' which, in Arabic, signifies 'Go, go,' but which he pronounced like 'Row, row.'   The words suited the emergency, and the Janissary was rescued from further bad treatment.

At a short distance from, and looking back on Safed, the view was really grand and beautiful. Beyond Tiberias rose a range of blue hills; the lake seeming to be close under the town of Safed. To the right, towering over all, was the old castle and its ruined walls; while the middle distance was varied by a succession of ravine, hill, valley, and field—the foreground consisting of abrupt, high, rocky banks, and a rugged, stony path, over which we were riding. A man held my horse while I sketched this glorious scene, for there was no time for dismounting.

Descending a very steep ravine, crossing narrow brooks, the water gushing over large stones, we came down on the Plain of Jordan, bounded by high hills, beyond which we saw Jebel-esh-Sheikh [1] (the Hermon of Holy Scripture), with patches of snow on its summit. This mountain, though mentioned often in the Old Testament, is particularly alluded to in Psalm cxxxiii., wherein 'that most excellent gift of charity,' the most difficult of all virtues to attain, is compared to the dew of Hermon, " that descends upon the mountains of Zion ;

---

[1] Jebel-esh-Sheikh is equivalent to 'Old Man's Mountain' —a name given from a fancied likeness to the white hair and beard of an old sheikh.

for there the Lord commanded the blessing, even life for evermore."

" The waters of Merom " (through which the Jordan runs to Lake Tiberias) were visible about an hour after we had entered the plain of Jordan, which was less cultivated than the country we had quitted.

We read of the lake of Merom in Joshua xi. 5, 7— " And when all these kings were met together, they came and pitched together at the waters of Merom to fight against Israel. So Joshua came, and all the people of war with him, against them, by the waters of Merom, suddenly, and they fell upon them."

The ground was here and there very marshy; and bad as the road was, when over rocky ground, it was to be preferred to the low swamps, in which the horses continually sunk, while the storks stood erect in the marshes, seeming quite astonished at the awkward proceedings of our struggling steeds. The heat in this plain was very great, and there was every appearance of an approaching tempest. We therefore prepared for it (having that of yester-day fresh in our minds); rode to a hill where the projecting rocks would, in a great measure, shelter us from the rain; and, placing saddles, cloaks, and bags in safety, remained there during the violent storm came up, producing the most beautiful effects.

Mount Hermon seemed to defy the mists which ran along the lower hills, and stood out clear and distinct among them, although every now and then its total disappearance seemed inevitable: clouds, heaped one upon another, obscured the sky, while loud claps of thunder were echoed and re-echoed among the more distant hills. When the weather looked somewhat settled, we pursued our journey. Finding the tents pitched on very boggy grass, we had them removed, much against the will of the muleteers, to (if not dry, at least) higher ground.

Next morning the sky was still cloudy, but though the day seemed unfavourable for the journey we thought it better to hasten on to Banias, which we hoped to reach before sunset.

Those parts of the plain over which we passed this day were but little cultivated. We frequently scaled large rocks, ascending hill after hill, then descending, had to struggle through morasses, out of which the horses with difficulty extricated themselves.

The monotony of the march was enlivened by meeting herds of buffalos, strings of camels (driven by fine-looking bedouins), and encampments of

Arabs, whose low huts were made of straw. During the day we passed near Kedash Naphtali, where Barak was born. It was one of the six cities of refuge.

The scenery improved towards the middle of the day, when we came to a very picturesque stone bridge, its masonry nearly hidden by small shrubs, flowers and weeds. The stream rushed rapidly on, bathing the willows and oleanders with which the banks on both sides were clothed. It was a beautifully cool and shady spot, to rest in after a ride of four or five hours.

I was at a short distance from my companions, sketching, when suddenly I heard a strange voice speaking Arabic. I looked up and saw an Arab standing by me, leaning on his gun. Finding I did not understand him, he joined the rest of my party, and, as I found afterwards, asked the gentlemen, if one of them was a doctor, as he was ill; unfortunately we could do nothing for him. In a few minutes a young woman with a pretty, golden-haired child in her arms came and sat by me. The mother had a very agreeable countenance. Her dress, which served as a petticoat and gown, over her full trowsers, was of very coarse white linen, with silver thread woven in it; the border had also a pattern of blue and silver thread; over all was a large, dark cloth jacket. Round her head was twisted a purple cloth, and hanging down her back, a thick white linen head-veil, with many plaits of hair flowing over her shoulders. She examined my dress very minutely; the white muslin sleeves pleased her, the tassels of my cloak surprised her, but when she saw the neck ribbon, she was perfectly enchanted, and as to the pocket-handkerchief she begged hard of me to give it to the lovely child. This I could not do, but I put the neck ribbon round its little throat, which delighted both father and mother; and the former took my hand and put it up to the child's mouth, who kissed it.

Continuing our ride to Banias we toiled up steep rocky paths, where we found trees and shrubs very abundant, particularly on grassy table land. We met people travelling, amongst whom were women on horseback wearing the curious horn, which is fixed on the front of the head and fastened behind. This *tantur* or horn, which is made of tin, silver, or gold, according to the rank or wealth of the wearer, and is sometimes a yard long, is shaped like a speaking trumpet. It rises from the forehead, and is fastened at the back of the head by a band. A large veil is thrown over it and falls down the sides of the head and shoulders. It is usually worn only by married women; but I believe unmarried women also occasionally wear it. There are many references to this horn in the Old Testament. It was sometimes worn by men. Job says "I have sewed sackcloth upon my skin, and defiled my horn in the dust," Job xvi. 15; and David alluding to the righteous, says, in Psalm cxii. 9, "His horn shall be exalted with honour." [1]

We were now not far from the site of Dan, which I regret we could not visit. Dan was called Laish, and became one of the seats of Jeroboam's idolatry. [2]

The situation of Banias is very beautiful; it is completely surrounded by hills; Mount Hermon rising immediately over it. There is also a castle in ruins, named Kalat Banias, on a hill of very considerable height, not far from the town. [3]

---

[1] When fastened on the head, this horn is like that of an unicorn.

"But my horn shalt thou exalt like the *horn of an unicorn*."—Psalm xcii. 10.

[2] Kings xii. 28, 29, 30.

[3] It stands on the top of a mountain, which forms part of the mountain of Heish, at an hour and a quarter from Banias; it is now in complete ruins, but was once a very strong fortress. Its whole circumference is twenty-five minutes. It is surrounded by a wall ten feet thick, flanked with numerous round towers, built with equal blocks of stone, each about

The vegetation was unusually rich; and there was a brook rushing by old towers and walls, and over foundations of ancient buildings, and great massive pieces of rock and stone scattered about, which almost impeded the course of this small, energetic stream, which was THE JORDAN. Tall trees mingled with the ancient ruins and modern town, and wild flowers peeped up among loose stones and hidden heaps of rock.

two feet square. The keep, or citadel seems to have been on the highest summit, on the eastern side, where the walls were stronger than on the lower, or western side. The view from hence over the Houle and a part of its lake, the Djebel Safed, and the barren Heish, is magnificent. On the western side, within the precincts of the castle, are ruins of many private habitations. At both the western corners runs a succession of dark, strongly-built, low apartments, like cells, vaulted, and with small narrow loop-holes, as if for musketry. On this side also is a well, more than twenty feet square, walled in with a vaulted roof at least twenty feet high; the well was, even in this dry season, full of water. There are three others in the castle. There are many apartments and recesses in the castle, which could only be exactly described by a plan of the whole building. It seems to have been erected during the period of the Crusades, and must certainly have been very strong. I saw no inscriptions, though I was afterwards told that there are several, both in Arabic and in Frank (Greek or Latin). The castle has but one gate, on the south side. I could discover no traces of a road, or paved way leading up the mountain to it."—*Burckhardt's Travels in Syria and the Holy Land.*

VOL. II.

Our tents were placed under a grove of olive trees—a more beautiful situation could not have been chosen—and from it, though surrounded by hills and much foliage, there was a charming view. Just below the tents was the Jordan with its thickly-wooded banks. Beyond, here and there, one caught a glimpse of some picturesque old buildings, shaded by olive-trees, and the whole was backed by grassy hills and trees which rose close to the town.

One of the sources of the Jordan is at Banias. We went, soon after our arrival, to the cave from whence it springs. It does not flow freely at first —stones impeding its rapid egress. We had now traced the holy river in all its length, from its mouth to its source.

" Stream most blest for His dear sake
　Who touch'd its sacred wave and hallow'd all its ground." [1]

Over the cave where the Jordan (which is there called Nas Mahr) rises at Banias, are small niches, in which, probably, statues were once placed. On a tablet near these niches is a Greek inscription.

Banias was called Cæsarea Philippi. It was when Jesus came into the " coasts of Cæsarea Philippi," that in conversation with Peter, our Lord said to him, " Thou art Peter, and upon this rock I will build my church, and the gates of hell shall not prevail against

---

[1] William's Baptistry, 'The Waters of the City of God.'

it," [1] words which have been so unfortunately strained by the Romish church to endue their spiritual rulers with absolute power. Cæsarea derived its name from the Emperor Tiberius, Philippi being added to distinguish it from Cæsarea on the coast; and it was afterwards called Neronias, in honour of Nero.

Under the Christians a bishopric was founded here, known by the name of Phœnicia.

It is said that the woman, on whom the miracle was performed when she touched the clothes of Jesus, mentioned in Matthew ix. 20., lived at Cæsarea Philippi. Eusebius, in his ecclesiastical history, relates that a brazen image of this woman stood near her house, representing her on a bended knee, with her hands stretched out like one imploring; and opposite this figure there was another, of a man standing erect, extending his hand towards the woman. This statue was intended for Jesus. The woman's name is said to have been Berenice. There was also a tradition, that at the base of the pedestal, on which the statue of the woman was placed, there grew a plant, which, rising as high as the hem of the brazen garment, was an antidote against all diseases.

[1] Matthew xvi. 18. [2] Translation of Eusebius' Eccl. Hist.

Beit-jenn was to be our next halting place. The day's journey to it from Banias was very fatiguing, and not so interesting as our rides had hitherto been. We passed close under the castle, after which the narrow path led us over rocky hills, and by sparkling brooks, with Mount Hermon on our left; and although the day was sunny, we felt the vicinity of snowy mountains. Riding alternately through bogs and over stony tracks, and descending into ravines and valleys, we entered an open space where thorny shrubs grew abundantly. We were now sonear the snow, that a servant rode up the side of the hill, and brought back a ball of it, which was a novel sight to us, as we had not seen any for six years. The guide appeared to admire it, for as soon as it passed into his hands, he conveyed it to his mouth, when it quickly disappeared.

During the day we heard a cuckoo; its cheerful note reminding one of spring—although in Syria one does not require to be told it is that happy season.

The rest of our journey was tedious, over the worst possible road. Towards night we encamped at Beit-jenn, on a dry, grassy hill, with a very wild view. Below us was a bright and lively streamlet, and a few flat-roofed huts placed among rocks;

behind were the mountains of Anti-Lebanon, the highest of which was nearly covered with snow. The road all the following day was at some distance from the range of Anti-Lebanon, and over unusually rocky ground. We had been grumbling at the latter, when suddenly we found ourselves sinking deeper and deeper into a bog, from which one of our party found it no easy matter to set his horse free. The guide did not escape so well; for as he got out of the swamp, his horse fell on its nose, and he upon his head, after which we complained no more of firm, rocky ground.

The prospect around us became more cheerful towards the middle of the day. From some rising ground, we could perceive a range of hills in the horizon, in the direction of Damascus, and every now and then we could trace a small river winding through the plain. We dismounted by a stream, and rested two hours under some willows during the middle of the day, reaching Artuz in the evening. Here the scenery was very pretty, and the river Seibarani flowed close to our tents: this was formerly supposed to be the Abana of Naaman,[1] but that stream is almost proved to fall into the Barada, near Fijah.[2]

---

[1] 2 Kings v. 12.
[2] 'Lands of the Bible,' Rev. Dr. Wilson, vol. ii., page 371.

It was a pretty ride, the next morning, from Artuz to Damascus. Corn-fields and olive-yards became numerous, and hawthorns, with their sweet blossoms, perfumed the air. "The walls of the gardens near Damascus are of clay, hardened in the sun, the bricks being each about a yard square, and formed, *in situ*, by the filling up of the clay within two boards placed parallel to one another as the building proceeds." [1]

We could not fail to remember, as we came near to the city, Saint Paul's journey from Jerusalem to Damascus, when "suddenly there shined round about him a light from Heaven; and he fell to the earth, and heard a voice, saying—'Saul, Saul, why persecutest thou me?'"

The approach to the city, coming from Jerusalem, is anything but imposing. On each side of a very long, ill-paved road, are miserable-looking houses (made of the same material as the walls of the gardens before-mentioned), and dilapidated mosques. I thought we must be in the suburbs; but as we rode on, we found that we were in the 'pearl surrounded by emeralds,' as Damascus has been called. This long paved road terminated in several narrower ones, in which butchers'-stalls were plentiful. We then entered the bazaar, under a roof which

[1] 'Lands of the Bible,' Rev. Dr. Wilson, vol. ii., p. 326.

must have been many feet above us, with shops on each side. Emerging from this covered place, through an archway with two doors—one very ricketty, the other prostrate—I thought we should now see palaces, gardens, and terraces, but there were still only poor looking dwelling-houses, which the minarets, near them, falling into decay, seemed ready to crush.

On we went, and entered a second very extensive covered bazaar. It was very dark and crowded, and my horse's head often rested on some turbaned gentleman's shoulders, who seemed quite accustomed to this, and merely looked at me while he moved, as well as he could, to one side, where probably he would meet another horse or donkey. I could scarcely look at anything, having to guide my horse through these dark passages. At length we arrived at our journey's end, and I was glad to dismount near a fountain in the courtyard of the hotel, into which I gladly entered, to find peace and repose in the cool, large, and beautiful room prepared for me.

The outside of the hotel did not promise well. Nowhere more than at Damascus must one attend to the old proverb, " Never go by appearances" —that is, as far as houses are concerned.

My room was as curious as it was handsome, large, and lofty, with a fountain in the centre. Steps on three sides led up to platforms, one of which was arranged as a sitting-room, the other two as sleeping apartments. The ceiling was about thirty feet high, of carved wood, painted red, green, and purple, and here and there gilt. To the height of about four feet, the walls were ornamented with beautiful coloured designs, and the floor in parts was of variegated marble.

The hotel was built round a court, in the middle of which was a large fountain, shaded by a few trees.

The *table d'hôte* was on a raised floor, open on one side to the court.

Quiet and repose were absolutely necessary, after a journey of eleven successive days on horseback, and I was thankful to be able to rest and try to gather strength for "sight-seeing" on the morrow.

CHAPTER XIII.

DAMASCUS lies at the foot of Anti-Lebanon. It
existed already in the days of Abraham,[1] and from
the first mention of it in that patriarch's time to the
conversion of St. Paul, it was the site of many important events spoken of in Biblical history. The
prophets foretold its destruction. Amos and Jeremiah spoke of the burning of Benhadad's palaces,
and of its later days. "Therefore, her young
men shall fall in her streets, and all the men of

[1] Genesis xv. 2.

war shall be cut off in that day, saith the Lord of hosts." Damascus fell in succession to the Babylonians, Persians, and Grecians, and had many different masters, including the Romans. In the time of St. Paul, it belonged to an Arabian Prince. It then became subject to the Greek emperors of Constantinople, and at last it was conquered by the Saracens. In 1301, Timour the Tartar attacked the city. Thus have the denunciations concerning it been fulfilled, and when we look at her fallen state, we may well exclaim, "How is the city of praise not left—the city of my joy."[1]

The bazaar, the interior of the private houses, and the window in the wall of the town, from which tradition says, St. Paul was let down in a basket, are the chief objects of attraction at Damascus. We went, of course, into the '*straight street*,' and the guides do not fail to shew the house where Ananias lived. The streets are narrower and, if possible, dirtier than those of Cairo and Jerusalem, and the pleasure of riding or walking is much diminished, if not entirely destroyed, by the butchers, who, if they do not actually kill the sheep in the streets, bring them immediately afterwards to where the passers-by must walk close to pools of blood.

[1] Jeremiah xlix. 25

Dogs are the scavengers, and are so numerous, and lie about so constantly in the middle of the streets, that one is always stepping aside to avoid treading on them. They have their respective quarters in the city, and will allow no dog to remain out of his proper division. I once saw an intruder hunted out with great barking and howling.

The bazaar is very extensive, and the same kinds of articles are sold there as at Cairo, and the scenes are similar, except that at Damascus there are fewer Europeans, and such a thing as a wheel carriage is never seen.

Separate localities are allotted to the different trades, as is usual in nearly all eastern cities. There was a long line of shops where merchants displayed their costly Damascus silks, some richly embroidered in gold or silver. Then we passed nothing but harness and trappings for horses, worked in shells and gold threads. At one place, ready-made apparel for women was suspended. Here was the coppersmith and the slipper vendor. There were enamelled pipes, embroidered tobacco-bags, guns, swords, and spears, some plain, some prettily inlaid. Then came the sweetmeat bazaar, where it was impossible to say whether children or flies were most numerous; and to this very eastern city, English prints and cottons have found their way in great abundance.

There is a ruin near the large mosque. It is very beautiful, but difficult of access, and can only be approached through a house at the back of the bazaar, the shops of which conceal the lower part of the columns. On ascending a staircase leading to the roof of a house, one is repaid by finding the remains of an ancient temple. Part of an architrave remains, and a few pillars are standing. The ornaments of the cornice resemble those I afterwards saw in the smaller temple of Baalbek. I sketched for two hours, forgetting the flight of time, and little heeding the impatience of my guide, who wanted to hurry me away.

The large mosque at Damascus, is said to occupy the site of the church formerly dedicated to St. John, but no stranger is allowed admittance. Not far from it is a very fine khan, where the travelling merchants deposit their goods. There is a large fountain in the centre. The ceiling is supported by granite pillars.

We visited some Jewish and Syrian families. The poor exterior of the houses belonging to the wealthy inhabitants would not lead one to expect such lofty, handsome and highly decorated rooms as are found inside. The houses are generally built round a large court-yard, in which there is always a fountain, often flowering shrubs of great beauty, and occasionally trees.

The ceilings and walls of the apartments are mostly of wood, painted in different colours, and frequently ornamented with much gilding, and inlaid with coloured marbles and mother-of-pearl; the beams being elaborately carved. The devices and patterns are very beautiful, and the colours most brilliant—some being turquoise blue, others green, red, or purple. In some rooms small mirrors were let into the wood-work, and round the cornices were bunches of grapes and leaves finely carved in wood, and gilt. Some of the divans were of rich embroidered silk, with raised flowers in gold, and bordered with deep gold fringe.

Like all eastern people, the inhabitants of Damascus are fond of European finery.

Among all this rich furniture, I saw tables covered with coloured glass ornaments, and many nick-nacks which looked quite out of place. In each house there was something new and amusing to see. At one, the Jewish maidens were washing the court-yard, which was full of water; and some were running nimbly along on their patterns, which are at least six inches high. At another, a lady met us with her hair dyed with henna. At a third, we saw an ancient dame with a singular head-dress; very small black ostrich feathers on each side, were hanging close to her cheeks; this, at a distance, gave her the appearance of having enormous whiskers—but seen nearer, she looked like an exceedingly old and strange bird.

Everybody who visits Damascus hears of the 'beautiful Esther;' and we were so luckly as to find her and her parents at home. After the murder of the monk, Tomaso, at Damascus, not many years ago, the story of which has been so often related by travellers, several Jews were tortured to make them give information as to who were the culprits. The father of Esther was one of those who underwent the most horrible sufferings. The Jewesses of this city shave off their eye-brows, and in their place paint long black and very arched streaks, higher or lower on their foreheads, as they think most becoming. These streaks meet each other over the bridge of the nose.

Esther is no longer young, but must have been very beautiful; her painted eye-brows did not improve her good looks. The dress of the ladies was very much like that of the Jewesses in the Holy

City. Esther and her mother led us up to the top of the house to shew us their handsome rooms.

The former walked easily up and down-stairs on her high patterns, which were much ornamented with mother-of-pearl. I then understood that they are not only worn by waiting-maids, but by all the ladies, who consider them the height of fashion.

As we entered some of the upper rooms in the Jewish houses, we saw small tablets fastened in the wall near the door, on which were inscribed sentences taken from the law.[1]

Damascus should be first seen from the road which leads from Beyrout. We rode out one day to the tomb called Rabbet-en-Nasr, where we staid some time; and, while looking down on the city, were fully occupied not only with its real story, but with the fables and legends relating to it; among the latter an old author, Maundrell, says, "It is related that Adam was formed of the red earth of the plain of Damascus;" and from near where we sat, Mahomet, before he commenced his extraordinary career, saw Damascus for the first

[1] " Therefore shall ye lay up these words in your heart, and in your s oul, and bind them for a sign upon your hand, that they may be as frontlets between your eyes."

" And thou shalt write them upon the door-posts of thine house, and upon thy gates.—Deuteronomy xi. 18—20.

time, and is said to have exclaimed, "Man can have but one paradise, and mine is fixed above;" so he turned away, and would not enter the city.

This earthly paradise, as Mahomet deemed it, is placed, as I have said, at the extremity of a large plain; its mosques, minarets, and flat-roofed houses being environed by verdant gardens and a mass of foliage, through which the glistening Barada is seen at intervals. As far as the eye can reach, we traced the direction of the route we had traversed since leaving Beit-jenn.

I cannot agree with those travellers who think Damascus so very beautiful, and certainly not with Mahomet that it is an earthly paradise.

It was a lovely day on which we left it; and, as we rode up the chalky hills where the tomb we had visited the day before stands, we turned round to take a last glance at the city. The road, as we descended on the other side, was slippery, and the horse on which my maid rode fell. She was very much hurt; fortunately, the litter was near, and she was placed in it; but there was no medical aid at hand. We had not gone far, however, when an English physician, who had been staying at Damascus, rode by. He kindly gave all the assistance in his power, and promised to visit the poor sufferer at our encampment at the end of the day.

This accident took away considerably from the pleasure of the journey. It was impossible not to be anxious, and we could not yet tell the extent of the injuries my maid had sustained.

For a great part of the day we rode by the side of the Barada, the banks of which were shaded by willows, poplars, and hawthorns. The road was, as usual, very rough, but the scenery was exceedingly beautiful, and occasionally grand; passing through ravines between bold rocky hills, we frequently crossed the narrow winding river, which rushed rapidly by, often precipitating itself over rocks in small cascades.

As we approached a most picturesque bridge with one arch, we came to a narrow gorge, near which was the site of Abila, [1] the capital of Abilene. Among the precipitous rocks of this narrow ravine are ruins and ancient tombs.

When we encamped for the night in the valley of Zebedani, I was thankful to find my maid better.

The plain in which we were was lovely; well

---

[1] Luke iii—1.

watered, and cultivated, and the orchards were in full blossom. There is a tradition that this beautiful vale is the site of Paradise.

The next morning, as we pursued our journey, the beauty of the country seemed to increase; vineyards, orchards, and hawthorns, with their fragrant flowers, were numerous; while on the highest range of Anti-Lebanon, lay the snow, as if it were still the month of December. On looking back on the valley, the fruit trees seemed also covered with snow, so thick were the white blossoms. As we neared the mountains which we were to cross in order to reach Baalbek, the plain became less fertile. We crossed many small rivulets, which were constantly fed in their passage by "steep falling torrents," that rushed down the sides of the hills.

The scenery, as we ascended Anti-Lebanon, became grand and imposing. After attaining a very considerable height, we saw the range of Lebanon rising beyond the valley in which Baalbek is situated; but our labours had only just begun, and for some hours longer we toiled up and down almost impracticable paths; our horses splashing through strong currents, that, impatient in their course, were

'Making sweet music o'er the enamell'd stones.'

Sometimes we rode over piles of rocks, then slid down over smooth, sloping, shiny slabs, or made our way through bushy thickets. At last we reached the highest point, where our horses scrambled over rocks and stones heaped upon each other, and we, at length, began to descend, and rode almost on to the very roofs of the houses of a village built on the side of a mountain.

We now looked down upon the valley, rich in pasturage and cultivation, where we intended to pass the night; but as yet there was no appearance of Baalbek, when an abrupt turn in the road brought us suddenly within sight of those magnificent 'temples of the sun.'

We approached from the side from which the ruins should first be seen. I fear there is often more than one likes to admit in the old saying, that 'first impressions are everything;' for I had felt before, in quitting Damascus, and looking back on it from the hill-side, that, lovely as it was, I should have found its beauty more striking, had I viewed it first from that same point.

Baalbek lies at the foot of Anti-Lebanon. When we arrived, the sun was setting, and part of the ruins were in deep shadow, while six strikingly-graceful, lofty columns retained their warm colouring, and stood out, relieved by the snowy-headed range of Lebanon, the highest points of which wore a pale rosy tint, thrown over them by the setting sun.

Below the spot from which we gazed at this lovely scene, was a little lively, purling brook, with one bank shaded by a group of poplars, and before us the stony road leading down to the ruins, where we hoped to find our tents; but they had not yet arrived, and did not come for a long and weary hour after we had dismounted. When they did come, the procession of horses and mules, laden with baggage, was led by the litter containing my poor maid, who had been again upset, but this time, fortunately, without injury. I sat on a rock till the tents were pitched, too tired that evening to look at or admire anything.

We stayed one entire day at Baalbek. I passed my time in exploring, or trying to sketch bits of the ruins at some little distance.

I could not decide at what time these fine temples were seen to most advantage—whether early, when the morning sun lit up the richly carved foliage of the capitals; at sunset, as I saw them yesterday; or by moonlight, when the six pillars looked even taller and more graceful than by day.

Baalbek is supposed to be alluded to in the eighth chapter of the Song of Solomon, under the name of Baalhamon. Josephus and Pliny mention Baalbek under the name of Heliopolis; but of the history of these temples but little is really known. There is a legend that they were built by angels at the command of Solomon.

Heliopolis has shared the fate of many other cities in Syria, having been pillaged by the followers of Mahomet, taken by the Crusaders, and sacked by Timour-beg, previous to its falling into the hands of the Turks.

The ruins are very extensive, consisting of a large and a smaller temple; of the former nothing remains but a colonnade with six pillars.

The roof of the smaller temple is gone, but the carvings of flowers, leaves, and fruit over the door leading into it are exquisite. The enormous size of the stones in some parts of the facing, intended to conceal, according to Wilson, the masonry on which the peristyles of the temple stand, is very striking; one was measured and found to be sixty-nine feet in length, thirteen in depth, and eighteen in breadth.

There are so many accounts of Baalbek, by different travellers, who have entered into minute

details of the rich and beautifully finished ornaments, and the perfect proportions of all parts
of these ruins, that it would be superfluous in me
to add any further description.

I had lately seen those gigantic and wonderful
works, the temples of Egypt. They seemed to me
as if raised by giants—such as the five Pandoos, to
whom the Hindoos attribute all gigantic under-
takings—but these at Baalbek, though no less vast
and stupendous, were in their effect light and graceful, as if they had been the work of fairies.

Our wanderings in Syria were now drawing to a
close; two days more, and we should be at Beyrout.

We continued in the "Lands of the Bible" till
we reached the shore of the Mediterranean, and I
felt every day more reluctant to leave a country
still "so full of hope and promise," and would
willingly, had it been possible, have retraced my
steps, and visited again all the places I had seen
since my arrival at Jaffa.

I feel sure that those who have enjoyed their
first visit to the Holy Land would more fully appreciate a second one; they would *see* more, *feel*
more, *think* more—in a word, realize more.

We crossed the range of Lebanon after leaving
Baalbek, and the scenery became grander every hour.

The second day we had a magnificent view of the Mediterranean in the direction of Beyrout, and the range of mountains on which we were seemed to extend into the very sea. The path was very steep, and full of large loose stones, which the peasants had thrown out of their fields, and our horses were in consequence tripping every minute.

The ravines and sides of the lowest hills were richly wooded, and at every turn of the road there were glorious prospects. We rode through every variety of beautiful scenery—along streams twisting and winding between low rocky banks; in narrow defiles, with rugged mountains towering up into the sky; through valleys and fields; by hills covered with pines; (here and there was a cedar of small size), and towards noon of the second day we descended to Beyrout, passing through shaded lanes. Among the trees were cactuses, and the beautiful *neem* (Indian lilac tree.)

Beyrout[1] is beautifully situated on the shore of the Mediterranean, at the distance of about four miles from the foot of Mount Lebanon. The view from the hotel was very fine. The snow on the

---

[1] It seems uncertain whether any place mentioned in the Bible can be identified with Beyrout. Dr. Robinson says it may be the Berothai of the Hebrew Scriptures. *Bib : Res :* vol. iii. pages 441, 442.

highest range of the Lebanon glistening in the noonday sun; the nearer mountains being well wooded up to their summits. Since Waee, in the Deccan, I had not seen such a landscape, combining every requisite for a lovely picture. During our short stay at Beyrout, I was unable to go out, having caught cold the last night of our tent life. I therefore passed the day sketching and looking at the enchanting view from the long gallery of the hotel. After two days' rest at Beyrout, we embarked on board a French steamer that was to take us to Alexandria.

I had been in many steamers in my time, and traversed many seas, seen many strange things, and stranger people, but the extraordinary *mélange* of human beings in *this* boat surpassed all I had ever met with. A steamer from one of these eastern ports is something like the toy called a ' Noah's ark.' You do not know what you may take out first—a dove or a lion—a lamb or a wolf. So in a steamer from the east, one has no idea what one may first light upon, whether a Sister of Charity returning to France, or an Arab bound to Mecca—a French countess, or a Scotch missionary.

All the European ladies were settling themselves in a very tiny cabin, and the greatest confusion prevailed—women, children, boxes, packages, trunks of all sizes, bags of all shapes, being crowded together in one indistinguishable mass. I peeped into the cabin, the door would scarcely open, and I retreated, hearing the cries of some young and refractory member of the society. I had a cabin to myself, having either by fair or unfair means ingratiated myself into the favour of the good stewardess, who gave me up her own. It was very small of course; but I was alone, and that is not a trifling comfort on board a steamer.

Dinner—a great event on board ship, and one which occupies the minds of many as soon as they have dispatched their breakfast (some persons when at sea thinking the miseries of the day are half over when dinner is announced)—was served as soon as we had weighed anchor.

What a society it was of which we had become members! One side of the steamer was occupied by Greeks and Turks, and the other side was given up to Christians. A cadi from Damascus took up his quarters on neutral ground, his carpet being spread in the middle of the deck, and close to the stern; his hareem was placed on the side next the Greeks and Turks.

The ladies of the hareem were completely separated from everybody, their retreat being protected by thick walls of canvass on all sides, except the one open to the sea.

How miserable this family looked! They were, including children, five in number. There was one large sofa, on which they sat huddled up together: on the ground were bedding, clothes, water-jars, and copper cooking vessels, all, *pêle-mêle*, untidy and dirty.

We touched at Jaffa the morning after leaving Beyrout. A great many persons came off, and the small vessel was soon filled to overflowing. All is so monotonous on board a ship, that the sight of a sea-gull, or a porpoise popping its head out of the water, affords a subject of conversation to the passengers for the rest of the day ; great, therefore, was the excitement when we heard that three horses were coming off from Jaffa. Two were hoisted up very successfully from the small and inconvenient boats in which they were brought, but as the third reached the side of the steamer, it began kicking furiously, and sprung into the sea. The side of the ship at which this took place was that occupied by the Greeks and Turks ; consequently, the Franks had to rush into their quarter to see the horses.

Everybody but myself ran to every *get-at-table*

place to see the horse splashing in the water. One
gentleman not being able to see, made a dart at the
back of the sofa, inside the hareem. I saw his wild
project, and that he meant to penetrate the canvass,
and suggested to him that it was not advisable to
invade the privacy of the Ottoman dames. He
heeded not my advice, and began climbing over;
but ere he had time to alight among them, a pierc-
ing scream caused him to make a hasty retreat.
As I was waiting for the result of his bold attempt,
and I knew indeed it would thus terminate, I was
much amused.

In the meantime, the poor scared horse had swam
out some little distance—the boats of the ship following it. At last one overtook it, and a man
caught its bridle; but the animal got away again,
was pursued, and at last caught by the tail; the reins
where also secured, and the sailors succeeded in keeping its head up as it swam along by the side of the
boat till it reached the steamer, when it was hoisted
on board quite exhausted.

The cadi had his mattress, with a cotton covering, spread over it. He was really as grave 'as a
judge.' He took no notice of his family, but sat
with his pipe (which an attendant frequently reple-
nished) by his side, and near him was an ample

supply of oranges. His dinner was brought to him by two of his servants. It was of a simple kind, but far from inviting. Before him was placed a black jar, and a black spoon, a tin mug, a plateful of meat cut up into large lumps—much like what would be given to a big dog—and which soon disappeared. In the black jar were curds and milk. Then this old gentleman performed his ablutions. A servant brought a large tin basin, and he proceeded to wash his face and hands—which certainly seemed to require the operation—a carpet was spread, and he began his prayers, bowing and prostrating himself in the direction of Mecca; this done, he was made very comfortable by his attendants, who arranged his pipe, and he sank down with his Koran in his hand, among his pillows, where he reclined till the time for his devotions again returned.

All the Mahomedans on board attended to their hours of prayer, which made Monsieur le Commandant say to me—"Ah! ces gens sont très RELIGIEUX, *ils sont très bien.*"

Amongst the passengers were two strongly-built Sisters of Charity, in long flannel robes, snow-white caps, and aprons. These ladies were accompanied by a 'lady superior,' tall, severe-looking, observing everything and everybody. There were travelling gentlemen with coats like bakers, and hats like coalheavers; a long, lank Presbyterian missionary looking very shy at a number of Roman Catholic priests. Then a line of Germans, Frenchmen, Englishmen, and Americans, all smoking pipes or cigars. There was a Jewish doctor of medicine, a French traveller from Abyssinia, families from Ceylon and Australia, and a youth who might have sat for the picture of ' Smike.'

I made acquaintance with an old French lady, who would know who I was, and insisted on having my ' carte de visite.' She was past seventy years of age; had ridden to Jerusalem 'pour faire ses pâques;' had been thrown from her horse, but was none the worse for it. She showed me all her treasures and relics, gathered in her journey. From her rosary was suspended a cross given her by a priest as a charm against lightning. Then a little piece of yellow wax blessed by another priest as a preventive of all mishaps " par terre et par mer." I thought it a pity she had not profited by this charm when she fell from her horse. I remarked to her that I concluded she did not really believe in the efficacy of these talismans. " Ah si, madame! tout est foi chez nous ;"

which I thought must be the case. Of course she had a piece of the real cross, and innumerable bits of saints' bones. Seeing I could not enter warmly into her feelings in regard to these matters, she held up her rosary, and shaking it triumphantly at me, cried out—"Ah, madame, vous n'avez pas de foi, vous n'avez rien du tout." I assured her that I had a great deal of faith, but that it was of quite a different nature from her own; but she left me, thinking, no doubt, I was a wretched unbeliever, and by no means a subject for conversion, in which latter surmise she was perfectly right.

At Alexandria, where our cadi, together with the other pilgrims to Mecca, left us, we heard news of the war with Russia; and our old friend, Abousaid, came on board to meet us, with a joyful countenance, saying—"All Greek here told to go: ' SHE ' go immediately."

On the voyage from Alexandria to Malta, there was very little that was interesting or amusing. The weather was bad; the ladies were ill; the children had fortunately no "*sea legs,*" and were kept below; the gentlemen consoled themselves with their cigars; the French lady with her relics; And when we arrived at Malta, all were in a hurry to land. Everybody was running against somebody else. Self alone was thought of, and the love of one's neighbour completely forgotten. When I came on deck in the morning I saw a very large package, quite six feet long, wrapt in a strong matting; on it, in large letters, was written "Madame la Supérieure." What can it be, thought I, it cannot be the lady herself? Then I thought it was a most gigantic violincello. I could not rest till I had solved the mystery. It turned out to be the mummy of a crocodile, which "Madame la Supérieure" was taking from Cairo as a souvenir to a friend at Antwerp!

After passing a few hours at Malta, we went on to Marseilles, where our pilgrimage and wanderings of many years terminated; and from thenceforth no new wares were added to the diverse contents of "the *Chow-Chow basket*."

APPENDIX.

Translation of the copy of the ancient record regarding the delivery of the Port and Island of Bombay by His Excellency Antonio de Mello e Castro of His Most Faithful Majesty's Council, Viceroy and Captain General of India, in the name and behalf of His Most Faithful Majesty Don Affonco, 6th, to Humphrey Cooke, Esq., Vice-Governor, for, and in behalf of His Serene Majesty Charles II., King of Great Britain, &c. &c.

(Extracted, by permission of the late Viceroy, Don M. de Portugal, from the Archives of Goa, and communicated by Major T. B. Jervis, F.R.S.)

In the Registry of the Royal orders for the year 1665, which is, in this Secretariate of State of India, in folio 54, is found together with a letter written by His Excellency the Viceroy Antonio de Mello e Castro in the said season to His Majesty, a treaty of the surrender and delivery of the Island of Bombay, in the following manner:

In the name of God, Amen. Be it known to all to whom this public instrument of the possession and delivery of the Port and Island of Bombay shall come, that in the year of our Lord 1665 in the 18th day of February of the said year, then and there being in the said Port and Island of Bombay, which is of the Jurisdiction of Bassein,—at the large house

of the Lady Donna Ignez de Miranda widow of the deceased
Dom Rodrigo de Moncato; present, Luis Mendes de Vas-
concellos of His Majesty's Council and Overseer of His
Majesty's Estates in India, and Doctor Sebastiao Alvares
Migos, Chancellor of the Court of Justice at Goa, the Ve-
readores and other officers of the Chamber of the said city of
Bassein, as also one Humphrey Cooke (which name in the
Portuguese or Spanish language would be *Inofre* Cooke)
Governor of the warlike men of His Majesty the King of
Great Britain, and Ensign John Torne and other persons of
the English nation, being all present with me, the undersigned
Notary Public. When it was declared by the said Luis
Mendes de Vasconcellos, and Doctor Sebastiao Alvares
Migos that, they had come there from the city of Goa, by
order of the Viceroy and Captain General of India, Antonio
de Mello e Castro, who had sent them, giving them two
letters from the King our master, and his, the Viceroy's,
directions: with the credential from His Majesty the King
of Great Britain, and the commission by which Sir Abraham
Shipman had made and appointed the said Humphrey Cooke
to succeed him on his death : all which are hereunder copied
as follows.[1]

No. 1.

I, Antonia de Mello e Castro Viceroy and Captain
General, &c., maketh known to all to whom this Alvara (or
instrument) may come, that, whereas, in conformity with
the order received from His Majesty to deliver the port and
town of Bombay unto the person nominated by His Majesty
the King of Great Britain, I have for this purpose appointed
and nominated Luis Mendes de Vasconcellos, &c., and Doctor
Sebastiao Alvares Migos. And, as it is expedient that, for
the better definition of all which on this occasion they shall

---

[1] Only a selection of these documents is here printed.

have to treat about, they should be invested with sufficient powers, such as the nature of the matter requires, and having full confidence in the abovenamed persons, that they will act in a manner most pleasing to His Majesty, and satisfactory to His Most Serene Majesty the King of Great Britain, I am pleased to grant unto them, and do hereby grant unto the said Luis Mendes de Vasconcellos and Sebastiao Alvares Migos, my full power and authority to determine upon, and remove, all and whatever doubts may arise, observing nevertheless the instructions I have ordered to be given them ; and every act of theirs conformable thereto shall have the same effect and validity as if done, determined and ordered by me. Provided, however, that in the event of any case offering where they cannot proceed agreeably to my order, they shall acquaint me with every particular, and with their opinion thereon, to enable me to resolve upon the same as may be most convenient.

I do accordingly notify to the Captains of the Cities of Chaul and Bassein, to the Factor and Judges thereof and to all other Ministers of Estates and Justice, officers and other persons whom this may concern ; and I do hereby order and direct them to comply with this Alvara, and to see that it is wholly and fully complied with, kept, observed and obeyed without the least doubt, &c., as if it were given in the name of His Majesty, &c., &c., &c.

Written by N. FERREIRA, at Panjin.

The 10th January, 1665.

No. 2.

To Antonio de Mello e Castro, &c.

MY FRIEND,—I the King send to you greeting. By the article of the contract which has been agreed on with the King of England, my good brother and cousin, concerning the dowry of the Queen his consort, my well-beloved and esteemed sister, which you will receive with this letter, you will understand why and how the port and country of Bombay belong to him, and the obligation I am under to direct the same to be delivered over to him. Immediately on your arrival at the States of India, you will ask for the credentials from the King, by which you may ascertain the person to whom possession shall be given, and make the cession. And you will accordingly cause the same to be made in the manner and form of that capitulation, observing the same yourself, and causing the whole and every part thereof to be duly observed: and that the whole may be committed to writing very clearly and distinctly, &c. And you will send the same to me by different conveyances, in order to settle and adjust the acquittance of the dowry promised to the King. By the other articles of that treaty it will be present to you the union we celebrated, and the obligation the King is under to afford me succour in all my urgencies and necessities, &c. &c.

(Signed)　KING.

Written at Lisbon, 9th April, 1662.

No. 3.

To ANTONIO DE MELLO E CASTRO,

Governor, &c.

MY FRIEND,—I the King send you greeting. By way of England intelligence reached me that in the States of India doubts have arisen with respect to the delivery of the town of Bombay to the order of the King of England, my good brother and cousin, in conformity with mine, which you carried with you. At which I was greatly surprised and much grieved; because, besides the reasons of convenience of this Crown, and more especially of the State of India, which made it necessary for me to take that Resolution, I wish much to give the King of England my brother every satisfaction. For these and other considerations, and as the King my brother must have sent fresh orders removing every doubt there might have originated from those he sent first, therefore direct and order that you do, in compliance with those orders of mine which you carried with you, cause to execute the said delivery punctually and without the least contravention, as the matter does not admit of any, and the delay is very prejudicial; and by your complying herewith as I expect, I shall consider myself well served by you, &c. &c. &c.

(Signed) KING.

Written at Lisbon, 16th August, 1663.

No. 4.

Articles by which Bombay was delivered by Antonio de Mello e Castro, Viceroy and Captain General, &c.

The island of Bombay shall be delivered to the English with a declaration, that, whereas the other islands under the jurisdiction of Bassein have through the bay of the said island of Bombay, their commerce, trade, and navigation with equal rights, liberty and freedom, the said English shall never prevent, nor cause any impediment thereto, nor levy any tribute or gabelle, neither on the exportation of salt or other merchandise of those islands, nor on any other articles that may be brought there from abroad. And it shall be free for all vessels loaded or empty, to navigate from the said islands, and territories of the Portuguese or other nations that trade with them. And the subjects of the King of Great Britain shall not oblige them to discharge or pay duties at their Custom-house, &c., and they shall enjoy good treatment, and free admission to the ports of our territories as they have hitherto enjoyed. That neither the port of Bandora on the island of Salsette, nor any other ports of that island shall be impeded, and all vessels from the said port or ports shall be allowed to pass and repass freely; and the English shall not allege that they pass under their guns, because it is on this condition that the island is delivered to them; and they cannot expect more than what is allowed them by the articles of the marriage treaty, &c.

That the English shall not receive any deserters from the Portuguese territory nor shall they under any pretence whatever conceal or protect them, as this is the most effectual means of preserving peace between the two crowns, and of avoiding future injuries; and they shall engage to deliver up all such deserters to the Captain, for the time being, of the city of Bassein. And as many Gentoos who may have in their charge goods and money belonging to Portuguese or other subjects of His Majesty, by way of retaining the same, may flee to Bombay and place themselves under the protection of the English flag, all such persons shall be apprehended until they shall satisfy the demands against them, or on their failing to do this, shall be delivered over to the Captain of Bassein, in order to satisfy the just claims of the parties whose property they have possessed themselves of.

That the English shall not interfere in matters of faith, nor compel the inhabitants of the island of Bombay to change their religion, or attend their sermons, and shall permit ecclesiastics to exercise their functions without the least impediment, this being a condition specified in the articles of peace under which the delivery of Bombay is made, &c.

That the fleets of the King of Portugal shall at all times have free ingress and egress into and from the said harbour of Bombay, &c.

That all persons who may possess estates on the island of Bombay, whether resident on the said island or residing elsewhere, shall be free to farm their estates or sell the same

on the best terms they may be able to v ... ...
the English require the said estates, they shall give for then
their fair and just value, &c. . .

That the inhabitants of the islands of Salsette and Caran-
jah and other places under the Portuguese shall freely fish
in the said bay and river, and the arm of the sea which
divides Bombay from Salsette, and the English shall not at
any time prevent them, nor shall the English at any time,
under any pretence whatever demand any tribute on this
account.

That the Carumbies, Bandaries or other inhabitants of
the villages belonging to the Portuguese shall not be admitted into Bombay, and all such persons resorting there shall
be immediately delivered up to their respective masters, and
the same shall be observed with respect to slaves who may
run away, and likewise with regard to artificers who may
leave the Portuguese territory and go to Bombay ; they shall
all be immediately delivered up ; and if the English should at
any time require the services of these artificers, they shall
apply to the Captain of Bassein, who will allow them for a
limited time, &c.

That in case any deserters from the Portuguese should offer
to change their religion and pass to the confession of the
English (to prevent them being restored to the Portuguese),
the said English shall not consent thereto ; and the same
shall be observed on the part of the Portuguese with regard
to persons who may desert to their territories.

That although the manor right of the Lady proprietrix of
Bombay is taken away, the estates are not to be interfered
with, or taken away from her, unless it be of her free will,
she being a woman of quality, they are necessary for her
maintenance. But after her death and when her heirs succeed to the estates, the English may, if they choose, take
them on paying for the same their just value, as is provided
in the case of other proprietors of estates ; and should the

... houses to build forts there-
... y pay their just value.

That persons possessing revenue at Bombay derived
either from Patrimonial or Crown lands shall continue to
possess them with the same rights as before, and shall not
deprived thereof, except in cases which the law of Por-
gal directs, and their sons and descendants shall succeed
to them, with the same rights and claims; and those who
may sell the said estates shall transfer to the purchasers the
same rights in perpetuity, that the purchasers may enjoy
the ' . , and their successors in like manner.

That the Parish priests, monks, or regular clergy
residing in Bombay shall have all due respect paid them as
agreed to, and the church shall not be taken for any use
whatever, nor sermons preached in them, and those who
may attempt it shall be punished in such manner as may
serve as an example.

That the inhabitants of Bombay and the landowners of
that island shall not be obliged to pay more than the foras
they used to pay His Majesty, this condition being ex-
pressly mentioned in the treaty.

That there shall be a good understanding and reciprocal
friendship between both parties, rendering one another every
good office, like good friends, as this was the object of deli-
vering this and other places, and the intention of His
Most Serene Majesty the King of Great Britain, as appears
by the treaty made and entered into by and between the two
Crowns.

ANTONIO DE MELLO E CASTRO.

Given at Panjin, 8th Jan., 1665.

"Possession was accordingly given and delive made of the port and island of Bombay, which comprehends in its territories the villages of Mazagon, Parell, Worlee, &c., and the said Governor Humphrey Cooke accepted and received the same in the name of His Serene Majesty the King of Great Britain, the manner and form laid down in the instructions from the Viceroy Antonio de Mello e Castro. By all and every declaration, clause, and condition in the said instructions, which are fully expressed and declared, he promised (in the name of His Majesty the King of Great Britain) to abide; and, saying, assuring, and promising so to do, he took personally possession of the said port and island of Bombay, walking thereupon, taking in his hands earth and stones thereof, entering, and walking upon, its bastions, &c., and performing other like acts, which, in right, were necessary, without any impediment or contradiction, quietly and peaceably, that His Majesty the King of Great Britain might have, possess, and become master (also his heirs and successors) of the said island.

And the inhabitants thereof, gentlemen and proprietors of estates within the circuit and territories of the said island, who now pay foras to the King our Master, shall pay the same henceforth to His Majesty the King of Great Britain. And the same L. M. de Vasconcellos, S. Alvares Migos and the Governor Humphrey Cooke, have ordered this instrument to be drawn up, and copies thereof given to parties requiring it, and that the same shall be registered in the book of the Tower of Goa, and in that of the Chamber of the city of Bassein, and of the factory of the said city, and at all other suitable places; and that the necessary declarations shall be recorded in those books, that at all times may appear the manner in which this possession was given and delivery made. And as they thus ordered this public instrument to be prepared, they, the said L. Mendes de Vasconcéllos, &c., &c., have put their names thereto in testimony of their having made the said delivery, and the Governor Humphrey Cooke, his, in testimony of his having accepted possession, &c., &c.

(Signed) ANTONIO MONTIERA DE FONCEÇA,

Notary Public of the city of Basseiu, &c.[1]

[1] Proceedings of the Bombay Geographical Society, Report on the Landed Tenures on Bombay, by T. Warden, Esq.—communicated by Major T. B. Jervis.

THE END.

LONDON:
Printed by Schulze and Co., 13, Poland Street.

Lightning Source UK Ltd.
Milton Keynes UK
UKHW022121060519
342211UK00007B/230/P